SECRET
LISBON

Jonglez

SECRET LISBON is a new type of guidebook. Its author, Vitor Manuel Adrião, has brought to light the very unique character of this city which, according to some, is destined to become the spiritual capital of Europe. This guidebook has thus been adapted to the city and, contrary to our other publications, contains numerous esoteric elements, making it a veritable guide of initiation. We have made a considerable effort to ensure that this information remains accessible for readers who are unfamiliar with this tradition. We have also tried to clarify things by adding several themed passages whose purpose is to provide the keys to understanding these topics which are too often impenetrable for the general public.

Like our other guides, *SECRET LISBON* also includes places, people and anecdotes that we hope will allow you to continue to discover the unusual, secret or unknown aspects of this capital city.

SECRET LISBON also shed light on the numerous yet overlooked details of places we pass by every day. These details invite us to pay more attention to our urban landscape and, more generally, to regard our city with the same curiosity and attention we often have when traveling.

Comments about the guidebook and its contents, as well as information on sites we haven't mentioned, are welcome.

Your comments will help us enrich our future editions.

Please contact us at:
• Jonglez Publishing, 17, boulevard du Roi, 78000 Versailles, France.
• by e-mail : info@jonglezpublishing.com

LISBOA

IC17
Paço do Lumiar

Av. Padre Cruz

Paiã

IC1

Brandoa

Pontinha

J

Amadora

Norton de Ma

Estrada de Benfica

Estádio da Luz
(Sport Lisboa
é Benfica)

d

Benfica

Ó
Un

R. C. Michaelis

Damaia

Jardim
Zoológico

Radial da Buraca

Buraca

Alfragide

IC19

Sete Ríos

Parque Florestal
de Monsanto

José

Estrada de Monsanto

Forte de
Monsanto

Camp

Estrada da Circunvalação

Márcos

A5 Av. E

Portela

Parque Florestal
de Monsanto

Ca
de C

Autoestrada do Oeste

Caselas

Alcântara
Palácio
Real das
Neces-
sidades

Estrada dos

Aqua
Parque

Tapada
da Ajuda

L

Estrada de Circunvalação

Caramão

Av. Infante Sant

Forte do
Alto de
Duque

Calçada da Ajuda

Av.

Ajuda

Avenida Dom Vasco da Gama

Restelo

Santo
Amaro

Belém

Estádio do
Restelo

Museu Nacional
dos Coches

A2

Mosteiro dos
Jerónimos

IP7 Ponte
25 de Abril

Avenida
da Índia

E01
E90

Torre de Belém

CONTENTS

ALFAMA - GRAÇA - MOURARIA

BAIXA - ROSSIO

CONTENTS

BELEM - SANTO AMARO - AJUDA

CONTENTS

ALFAMA - GRAÇA MOURARIA

THE UNUSUAL CAPITALS OF LISBON CATHEDRAL ❶

Largo da Sé
• Opening times: Monday to Saturday, 10am to 6pm
• Bus: 37

The construction of the Sé (cathedral) of Lisbon, the work of the 12th-century master of the Builder-Monks Frei Roberto de Lisboa (see hermetism, p. 60), began in Roman times and was completed in the Gothic period. Stunning Roman capitals adorn both sides of the central door of the cathedral's main entrance.

> *Not just a symbol of the struggle between Christians and Muslims ...*

One capital shows two knights fighting, one astride a lion and the other astride a bull – a rather strange representation of the *psychomachia*, the moral struggle between Christians (the bearded knight and the lion are linked to the Light, the Sun, and Christ) and Moors (illustrated by the beardless knight and the bull, whose horns represent the crescent moon, the symbol of Muhammad). Beyond this simple allegorical interpretation, this strategic struggle is also viewed as an expression of the cosmic cycle of the Earth led by the Sun and the Moon, which illustrates the very essence of Life and Death. This astronomical/astrological character, marked by the opposition between the signs of the Lion and Bull (Taurus), also designates the presence of the mixed, or androgynous, forms of worship that were celebrated in this cathedral. One form was of a public nature (Catholicism, represented by the Lion of Judah), while the other was more secret, but also supposedly celebrated here. It is represented by the Bull, a symbol of the secret or primordial Tradition (see the Holy Grail, p. 20).

The Archangel Michael, represented on one of the nearby capitals, mediates the union between the Lion of Judah and the Bull of Ishmael (Islam is descended from Ishmael, whose tribe had a coat of arms featuring a bull, which is also a symbol of the occult forces of spiritual power). In this context, the presence of Archangel Michael symbolises the union of Tradition and Religion, and, by fighting the dragon (which is associated with Muslim heresy), he is also a reminder of the fact that this now Christian cathedral was once the Islamic mosque of *Al-Usbuna* (Arab Lisbon).

PRINCIPLES OF SACRED ARCHITECTURE

A well-to-do man strolling through a quarry came across a group of three workers. He asked them what they were doing. "I'm earning a living," the apprentice replied. "I'm cutting stone," the journeyman answered. The third man, the master builder, looked at the stranger with disdain and declared: "I'm building a cathedral."

Keepers of the hermetic notions of sacred geometry (see p. 202), the basis of sacred architecture, the medieval Builder-Monks constituted the first *operational* (or *cooperative*) Builders Guilds that built Europe's principal Roman and Gothic monuments, and particularly the grand cathedrals. The latter were conceived so as to reproduce the Universe, so that what is above (in Heaven) is identical to what is below (on Earth) and vice versa. Although temples are a static form of celestial movement, they are nevertheless animated by the presence of the faithful.

The design of the temple floor is a well-ordered, horizontal projection of the Universe. According to solar orientation, each cardinal direction indicates an extreme position of the seasonal and daily cycle and places the temple in a harmonised movement with Space. The temple's journey reproduces the solar year, punctuated by the façades, on a path that leads from the Shadows to the Light.

In Judaeo-Christian tradition, Autumn, or Twilight, is to the west; Winter, or Midnight, is to the north; the Dawn or Daybreak of Spring is to the east; and, finally, Summer, or Noon, is to the south. This dynamic of space is used in the liturgical calendar, as depending on the period of the ritual year some doors are opened while others are closed, following the symbolism of "Holy Doors". The north is the darkest part of the temple. It expresses the cold, the shadows, and the invisible world that the subterranean world, or crypt, represents. All the symbolism of the north door is consecrated to the stellar origins, or the North Star.

The east indicates the beginning of the World. It is from this direction that the Sun rises, its first ray landing on the altar. It also shows the way to Jerusalem, and more importantly, Heavenly Jerusalem (a symbol of paradise). By focusing the power of the Rising Sun, it makes it shine like Life throughout the temple. The south marks the solar zenith, the height of Creation and its fructification. It is thus where the pulpit and the Gospel, the manifestation of the Holy Word, are placed. The west is the area of contemplation and Death, where profane and sacred meet. The main entrance is always placed to the west so mortals can reach the immortality symbolised by the altar, to the east. The west represents Autumn, the End of Time, and the end of a planetary cycle marked by the zodiac, represented here, at the centre, by the Holy Father (who symbolises the central Sun), or by the Son surrounded by the twelve apostles.

Following the *decumanus* (east to west) and the *cardo* (north to south) (see p. 89), there are two entrances to the temple. The main entrance is called the *Door of Time* because it indicates the Sun's path through the nave from east to west, thus starting Time in the sacred Space. The *decumanus* determines the human axis of the edifice, from birth to death, or east to west. Entering by the west door allows Time to move from Life to Death or, in other words, from the neophyte who enters the temple from the exterior, to the initiate who participates in the Primordial Origin as symbolised by the main altar to the east.

A side entrance, called the *Door of Eternity*, placed in relation to the *cardo* (or north to south) is also very common. The *cardo* represents the axis of Eternity and crosses the *decumanus*, which represents Time. Thus, the Time of Eternity is located beneath the vault's keystone, the philosopher's stone or cornerstone of the temple.

As the temple is the static manifestation of the Body of God, its *outline* represents a human body, with its arms in the shape of a cross or along its body. Each part of the temple possesses properties that can be assimilated to the human body. The circle of the apse represents the head; the crossing of the nave and the transept symbolises the heart, or the life that beats throughout the temple. As for the west façade, it represents the feet of the Body of God, thus reproducing and summarising the principles and functions of the entire building. Neophytes are informed of the spiritual journey they will embark upon by reading the west façade. The "feet" of God also evoke those of the faithful entering His Home in order to find themselves through the Grace of the Holy Spirit.

This entire arrangement creates a state of "vibrant sympathy" between Man and the Cosmos. Entering the temple is like entering the human body, in other words an act of *introspection*. In fact, it is the execution of a principle of Judaeo-Christian tradition found in the hermetic phrase "know yourself and you will know the Universe and the Gods".

LISBON CATHEDRAL'S "HOLY DOOR"   ❷

Largo da Sé
• Opening times: Monday to Saturday, 10am to 6pm
• Bus: 37

Reminder of the passage of the Holy Grail?

A n earthly expression of Heaven's Gate, guarded by the Archangel Michael, the Holy Door symbolises the passage between the human realm and the realm of Heaven. Opened only on certain days fixed by the religious calendar, such as for the *Jubilee*, the door plays a highly important role, which is why only the most important Christian temples that strongly abide by its spiritual foundations have Holy Doors.

Contrary to popular belief, it is not just the four basilicas of Rome that have Holy Doors. Upon entering Lisbon Cathedral, a discreet inscription can be seen on the left confirming the existence of a Holy Door. Outside, the other side of the door is to be found along rua do Aljube on the north side of the building.

The reasons for its existence are as rare as they are vague. The only certainty is that the door gives access to the inside of the church as well as to the Cardinal Patriarch's lodge through another small side door located in a hidden corner of the main door.

Following the creation of the Lisbon Patriarchate on 3 November 1716, the Portuguese Patriarchate esteemed that, as Saint Peter's in Rome had a

Holy Door, then Lisbon Cathedral should have one as well. This claim was probably also supported by the mysterious legend according to which the Holy Grail itself (the receptacle for Christ's blood and the Virgin's tears) had supposedly passed through this door several centuries before (see p. 20). Taking advantage of the construction of the Patriarch's lodge in early 1717, they annexed the Holy Door, an action which attests to the Portuguese Church's desire to free itself from the politics of the Roman Church. "The Romans have one, and so do the Portuguese", they seemed to declare.

The first Holy Door appears to have dated from the 12th century when Bishop Diego Gelmírez inaugurated the Cathedral of Santiago de Compostela's Holy Door on the occasion of the Holy Year (25 July 1101). It was not until 1499 that the Pope opened a Holy Door in Rome, most certainly inspired by the other one in Jerusalem. This door, more commonly called the "Sun Door" (or "Golden Door" or "Lion's Door"), is supposedly the door through which Jesus passed on Palm Sunday and where, according to religious tradition, the next Messiah should enter.

This tradition is linked to the *Jubilee* celebration (celebrated every 25 years since Pope Boniface VIII first celebrated it on 22 February 1300), which occurs in a Holy Year. On this occasion, the Pope or the Patriarch opens the Holy Doors. Lisbon Cathedral's *Jubilee* began to be celebrated in 1717, the year the Lisbon Patriarchate was founded.

Symbolically, the Holy Door represents *Mary*, or the "Heavenly Gate" (*Portae Coelis*), as shown by the *fleur-de-lis* carved on the outside of the door and which signifies *Divine Royalty*. Passing through this Holy Door, that only the Cardinal Patriarch can open and use, symbolises the transition from mortality to immortality.

Finally, the Greek letters *Alpha* and *Omega*, also engraved on the door, symbolise the "Beginning" and the "End" and represent the Omnipotent God, Lord of Life and Death, through whom all things were created and will be reassembled, according to Saint John the Apostle in the New Testament (Revelations 1:4-8), and the Prophet Isaiah (44:6-8) in the Old Testament. In the Middle Ages, *Alpha* and *Omega* often decorated the Judge of the Universe's halo, to the right and left of his forehead. These two Greek letters are also commonly used to ornament Christian tombs to indicate that the person resting below saw his beginning and end in God.

THE MYSTERY OF THE HOLY GRAIL

In Western spirituality, the *Holy Grail* or holy vessel (*Saint Vaisel*) is the chalice in which Jesus drank during the Last Supper, before suffering on the Cross, and is also what Joseph of Arimathea used to collect the Saviour's Royal Blood.

According to the Initiatory Tradition, after the tragedy of Calvary, the Holy Grail was kept in seven temples in Asia, to which Saint John the Apostle made mention in a way as the "seven churches of the Orient". Around AD 985, it travelled to seven cathedrals in the West, then continued towards the fifth continent, South America, or Brazil to be more precise. The seven cathedrals which, according to the Tradition, supposedly had a link to the Grail were the following: 1) Westminster Abbey, London, England; 2) Papal Basilica of Saint Mary Major, Rome, Italy; 3) Basilica of the Holy Blood, Bruges, Belgium; 4) Santa Maria Maior (Sé Patriarcal) Cathedral, Lisbon, Portugal; 5) Cathedral Church of Saint Peter and Saint Paul, Washington DC, United States; 6) Mexico City Metropolitan Cathedral, Mexico; 7) Cathedral Basilica of Salvador, São Salvador da Bahia, Brazil.

In the Middle Ages, the Holy Grail myth became linked to the legend of King Arthur and the 12 Knights of the Round Table who searched for this Chalice. Although the Arthurian legend did not take its literary form until the end of the 12th century with the poetic works of Chrétien de Troyes, it had spread through all of Europe much earlier thanks to the itinerant bards, or troubadours and minstrels, protected by the Knights Templar. The legend's birthplace was not exactly Celtic Brittany, but Moorish Sintra, a mountainous region reputed to be sacred. In fact, the Moors had brought the worship of the *Coupe Djin* or *Divine*, which was related to the worship of King Solomon, to this region in the 8th century. Count Henry of Burgundy, the father of Dom Afonso Henriques, learned of this tradition from Islam in 1095 during the conquest of Sintra, a city he later lost to the Almoravids. It was not until 1147, thanks to Afonso Henriques' army and the help of the Knights Templar, that Sintra definitively became Christian and an integral part of this *Porto-Graal*, the name given to this burgeoning country by the king.

According to its Greek etymology, the word *Graal* comes from *kratale* and *kratêr* and has undergone numerous transformations: from *graalz*, or *grazale* (Provençal) meaning "plate", to the Latin (it is supposed) *gradalis*,

meaning "plate one uses gradually" or several times, to the derivations *grato* (liking) and *agradar* (to please), the latter being the courteous interpretation that has survived to the present day. Furthermore, *Saint-Graal* (Holy Grail in French) may also be a derivation of *Sangue Real* or *Sang Royal* (the Royal Blood of Jesus Christ, of the royal line of David and Solomon), which was transformed into *San Greal* and then to

Saint-Graal. It signifies a cup, chalice or plate on which the chalice is placed. It has also been associated with a Celtic cauldron, alchemical glass, and even the life-giving uterus of a woman, which is represented in nature by the sacred grotto.

Etymologically, there is also a difference between *Gral* and *Graal*. The *Gral* is the mortar, the laboratory object used to prepare certain chemical mixtures. The *Graal* is the Holy Cup and, naturally, it is used to make the most sublime, spiritual and mystical alchemical fusions and sublimations. The dominating influence of the Holy Grail can thus be noted in several traditions:

The **theurgical tradition**, in which the Holy Grail mysteries are synonymous with the Initiatory Tradition.

The **Byzantine tradition**: elements of the Byzantine rite of the Procession of Saint John Chrysostom are equivalent to elements of the Procession of the Holy Grail, notably associating the Fisher-King to Christ, the Priest to the Holy Spirit and the Sacristy to the "Grail Chamber".

The **druidic tradition**, which searches for the origins of the Grail in fertility rites and the Eleusinian Mysteries.

The **Judaeo-Christian tradition**, which connects the Grail to the relics of the Old Testament that were later transformed into Christian symbols.

The **Persian tradition**, which identifies the Grail Castle as the *Takt-i-Taqdis* or "Throne of Arches" a palace that King Khosrow II (590-628) ordered to be built in Persia; and which sees the Grail in the disk or engraved plate of an allegory of the Persian castle (now on display at the National Museum of Berlin).

The **Egyptian tradition**, in which the Grail Castle is identified as the Ark or funerary boat holding the 14 pieces of Osiris that Isis recuperated.

The **Islamic tradition**, which, by interpreting the Grail symbolism according to its own esotericism, or Sufism, equates it to the *Djin* vase.

The **Gnostic tradition**, in which the Grail is equated with the *Sacrum*, or the sacred symbol representing the Mystery of the Most Holy Trinity.

The **hermetic tradition**, in which the Grail is associated with the doctrines of Hermes Trismegistus, as illustrated in his works *Corpus Hermeticum* and *Emerald Tablet*.

The **Cistercian tradition**, whose monastic ideals were highly influenced by the ideology contained in the *Queste del Saint Graal* (Quest for the Holy Grail).

The **Templar tradition**, which was linked to the worship of the Royal Blood and the risen Christ and which widely spread the Cistercian monk Joachim de Flore's *Nuevo Evangelio* (New Gospel).

The **chivalrous tradition** from which the Holy Grail tradition ensues, and which is revealed in works such as the *Quatro Livros de Linhagens*, *Nobiliários* and *Amadis de Gaula*, among others. Medieval troubadour Wolfram d'Eschenbach called it the "Stone of God" and the alchemists later called it the "Philosopher's Stone". In other words, they identified the veritable spiritual realisation of Man as the supreme purpose of the quest for the Holy Grail.

HOW LUSITANIA BECAME PORTUGAL

Lusitania (*Luxcitania* in Latin, meaning "place of light") is the name given by the classical authors of antiquity to the territory located in the west central region of the Iberian Peninsula where the Lusitanian people lived. This civilisation began to evolve at the end of the Neolithic period, reaching its peak in the Iron Age. The Romans occupied the peninsula at some point during the second Punic war (218-201 BC) and established their capital at Mérida (*Emerita Augusta* in Latin).

Lusitania roughly covered what is now the Portuguese territory south of the Rio Douro, Spain's Extremadura and part of the province of Salamanca. It became part of the Roman province of Hispania Ulterior, then an autonomous province in 29 BC, until its detachment from Rome, when it fell into the hands of the Alani people in AD 411.

The Lusitanians were a mix of Celts from northern Europe and Ligurians who came from the southern part of the Italian peninsula by way of the Mediterranean Sea, even if the anthropological base of this ethnicity is to be found in the Iberians, the prehistoric civilisation that gave its name to the peninsula.

This "place of light" was so named for two basic reasons. First, Europe's largest vein of gold, exploited by the Romans, was found here. More importantly, since the Palaeolithic period, the Iberian Peninsula, or more precisely Sintra, to the west of Lisbon, had been Europe's unique vital centre among the seven centres that led the ancient world (according to tradition, in Peru, Mexico, North America, Australia, Portugal, Egypt, and India).

Graeco-Roman mythology also attributed a divine origin to the Lusitanian. He was a descendant of Luso, son of Bacchus or Dionysus (Mercury) and his wife Lyssa (Venus), the head of Bacchus' priestesses (the bacchantes). Luso was the fruit of their union and he, himself, had many sons – the Lusitanians. Moreover, in the 16th century, Gil Vicente affirmed that Lusitania was also the daughter of Lisibea (Lisboa) and the Sun. A Greek knight named Portugal supposedly fell in love with her. They married and went to live in Serra da Solércia (Sintra), leaving many descendants – the Portuguese.

History also tells of the Condado Portucalense (an earldom), stretching from Galicia to Coimbra, and which king Dom Afonso VI offered to Count Henry of Burgundy at the end of the 11th century. The latter occupied the territory and named it Porto-Galo, "place of roosters", or, in other words, of the Francs or French counts who had come from Burgundy to help the Christians to take back the Iberian Peninsula from the Moors. Dom Afonso Henriques, Portugal's first king and the son of Count Henry, would extend the borders of the Condado Portucalense, free it from the king of León and Castile in 1128, and elevate it to the status of a country (1139), making it the oldest country of feudal Europe by almost 500 years.

To the names Porto-Galo, Portucale and finally Portugal, Afonso Henriques added the name Porto-Graal, as is marked on the document with which he gave Tomar to the Knights Templar. Early on, he had dedicated the country to Christ and Saint Mary, the expression of the Holy Spirit, and he thus considered it to be the seat of the geopolitical evolutions that would spread to the rest of the continent.

THE SACRED SYMBOLISM OF THE *FLEUR-DE-LIS*

A symbol of Lisbon (*Lis Boa* or *Boa Lis*, as chronicler Fernão Lopes called it in 1434), the *fleur-de-lis* is symbolically linked to the *Iris* and the *Lily* (*Lilium*). According to Miranda Bruce-Mitford, Louis VII the Younger (1147) was the first king of France to adopt the iris as his emblem and use it as a seal for his letters patent (decrees). As the name *Louis* was then spelled *Loys*, it supposedly evolved to "*fleur-de-louis*", then "*fleur-de-lis*", its three petals representing Faith, Wisdom and Courage.

In reality, even if there is a strong resemblance between the iris and the fleur-de-lis, the French monarch merely adopted an ancient symbol of French heraldry. In AD 496, an angel purportedly appeared before Clotilda (wife of Clovis, king of the Francs) and offered her a lily, an event that influenced her conversion to Christianity. This miracle is also reminiscent of the story of the Virgin Mary, when the Angel Gabriel appeared to her, holding a lily, to tell her she was predestined to be the mother of the Saviour. This flower is also present in the iconography of Joseph, Christ's father, to designate him as the patriarch of the new holy dynasty of divine royalty.

In 1125, the French flag (and coat of arms) depicted a field of *fleurs-de-lis*. It remained unchanged until the reign of Charles V (1364), who officially adopted the symbol to honour the Holy Trinity, thus deciding to reduce the number of flowers to three. The flower's three petals also referred to the Trinity.

The lily stylised as a *fleur-de-lis* is also a biblical plant associated with the emblem of King David as well as Jesus Christ ("consider the lilies of the field ..." Matthew 6:28-29). It also appears in Egypt in association with the lotus flower, as well as in the Assyrian and Muslim cultures. It became an early symbol of power and sovereignty, and of the divine right of kings, also signifying the purity of body and soul. This is why the ancient kings of Europe were godly, consecrated by the Divinity through sacerdotal authority. Thus, theoretically, they were to be fair, perfect and pure beings as the Virgin Mary had been, she who is the "Lily of the Annunciation and Submission" (*Ecce Ancila Domine*, "Here is the Servant of the Lord," as Luke the Apostle reveals), and patron saint of all royal power.

The lily thus replaced the iris, which explains why, in Spanish, "*fleur-de-lis*" becomes "*flor del lírio*", and why the two flowers are symbolically associated with the same lily.

Botanically, the *fleur-de-lis* is neither an iris nor a lily. The iris (*Iris germanica*) is a plant of the Iridaceae family that originates in northern Europe. The more commonly known lily species (*Lilium pumilum*, *Lilium speciosum*, *Lilium candidum*) are members of the Liliaceae family that originates in Central Asia and Asia Minor. The true *fleur-de-lis* belongs to neither the Iridaceae nor the Liliaceae family. It is the *Sprekelia formosissima*, a member of the Amaryllidaceae family that originates in Mexico and Guatemala. Known in other languages as the Aztec lily, the São Tiago lily, and the St James lily, *Sprekelia formosissima* is the only species of the genus. It was named in the 18th century by botanist Carl von Linné when he received a few bulbs from J. H. Van Sprekelsen, a German lawyer. The Spanish introduced the plant to Europe when they brought bulbs back from Mexico at the end of the 16th century.

The monarchs and princes of Portugal knew of its symbolic meaning much earlier, however, since, roughly from the time of Afonso Henriques, and especially at the end of the 13th century, the lily, converted or stylised into the *fleur-de-lis*, appeared prominently on Portuguese coats of arms, with all its inherent, immediate and essential symbolism. This was entirely thanks to the Arab influence that brought it from Egypt to the Iberian Peninsula during the occupation.

Pour bîẽ

THE PENTAGRAMS OF THE CATHEDRAL CLOISTER

❸

Largo da Sé
- Open Monday, 10am to 5pm ; Tuesday to Saturday, 10am to 7pm
- Bus: 37
- Tram: 12 or 28

> *The magic symbol of a medieval exorcism*

The construction of Lisbon Cathedral's cloister, which is built in two architectural styles, Roman and Gothic, began during the reign of Dom Dinis (1279-1325). Above the arches can be found rosettes carved in the form of crosses, six-pointed and especially five-pointed stars.

The five-pointed star, or pentagram (which is represented in the same number of candleholders in front of the temple's main altar), is particularly significant here. In Christian iconography, it refers to Christ's five wounds on the Cross, but, due to its closed form, it is also identified with the circle represented by the coming together of the beginning and the end in Christ.

For the medieval Builder-Monks (see hermetism, p. 60), the *pentagram* signifies the *realisation*, the expression of the *perfect*, to the point that it became the sign of mutual recognition for the members of architectural guilds. They would draw the symbol on their letters as a form of salutation. The symbol's meaning was equivalent to that of the Latin word *vale* (be well) or *higia*, from the Greek goddess of health Hygia or Hygieia.

Here, the pentagram marks not only the productive presence of the medieval Builder-Monks, but is also the magic symbol of exorcism and protection against malicious influences, both visible and invisible. In the Middle Ages, it was a powerful talisman that represented Christ the Omnipotent, the Living God Himself, before which the malicious shadows revealed their impotence.

That is why the pentagram was used here as the protective symbol of the cloister, an expression of paradise or the "Heavenly Jerusalem".

Through its square form open to the celestial vault, the cloister represents the union between the Earth and the Heavens, symbolising Man's closeness to God.

Before the archaeological digs, a well and a tree stood in the garden at the centre of the cloister. The well represented the subterranean world, while the tree represented the celestial world.

The cloister thus illustrated the three levels of the cosmic centre of paradise or "Heavenly Jerusalem" (subterranean, terrestrial, celestial) and was protected by the pentagram representing Christ.

THE BIRD PILLAR IN THE CATHEDRAL CLOISTER

❹

Largo da Sé
- Open Monday, 10am to 5pm ; Tuesday to Saturday, 10am to 7pm
- Bus: 37
- Tram: 12 or 28

Birds, messengers of the holy word

One of the sculpted capitals in Sé Cathedral cloister shows two birds drinking from a goblet. According to the Santa Cruz de Coimbra monastery's *Livro das Aves* (Book of Birds) and all medieval bestiaries, including Islamic bestiaries, birds are the messengers of the holy word (see also Ecclesiastes 10:20).

In Roman art, birds feed on holy bread (gnosis) and royal blood (illumination) – a reference to the Eucharist – in the holy vessel (*Saint Vaisel*). Thanks to the art of troubadours and minstrels, medieval spirituality celebrated this vessel under the name of the Holy Grail (see p. 20).

On this capital, one bird raises its beak while swallowing holy bread, thus illustrating how the soul rises towards the mysteries of God's wisdom. The other bird drinks royal blood from the goblet, thus showing the same soul embodied by the grace of the Holy Spirit.

PILLAR OF THE SOULS

Sé Cathedral cloister
Largo da Sé
• Open Monday, 10am to 5pm ; Tuesday to Saturday, 10am to 7pm
• Bus: 37
• Tram: 12 or 28

A symbol of the ascension of human souls

I n Sé Cathedral cloister, built in the 13th century under the reign of Dom Dinis, a strange Gothic pillar shows carved figures rising in a spiral manner from the base to the top.

Taken from one of the cloister's deconsecrated chapels, the pillar is a symbol of the ascension of human souls from the Earth to the Heavens. These souls, depending on the amount of virtue they possess, are in constant danger

of falling into hell, or, at best, of spending an indeterminate period of time in purgatory. The *Pillar of the Souls* also shows the four social classes of the Middle Ages (clergy, nobility, bourgeoisie, and the peasants) as they begin the St James' Way pilgrimage from Lisbon to the Cathedral of Santiago de Compostela in Spain, which was the most important pilgrimage at the time. All social classes participated – priests and bishops, kings and nobles, but most of all the lower classes. They all tried to pay for their sins and obtain indulgences.

SAINT ANTHONY'S LISBON MIRACLE 6

Largo de Santo António da Sé
• Bus: 37

> **When Saint Anthony saved his father from hanging**

Saint Anthony is undoubtedly the best-loved saint in Lisbon. His memory, closely held by all Lisbon residents, is revived by the numerous relics relating to him and which can be viewed at the Antoniano museum, next to the church, on the *Largo* that bears his name near Lisbon Cathedral.

Born in Lisbon in 1195, it is said that he was born here, in the very crypt above which his church stands. His parents had him baptised at Lisbon Cathedral a week later. His father, Martinho Taveira de Azevedo, a rich nobleman who served at the Senate of Lisbon, and his highborn mother, Teresa Bulhões, named him Fernando de Bulhões e Taveira de Azevedo. He dedicated his life to religion early, becoming the disciple, friend and confidant of Saint Francis of Assisi. He settled in Padua, Italy, where he died and where his relics became the object of a very important pilgrimage. A high priest, Santo António was a sage and was one of the Doctors of the Church, but he earned his reputation mainly through his exceptional miracle-working abilities.

Legend says that Saint Anthony saved his father from hanging here, on

Sé square. He was in Padua, preaching, when he suddenly felt that his father was in danger in Lisbon. In front of the congregation, he gathered his thoughts and miraculously appeared at the same moment in Lisbon, where his father was about to be hung after having been unjustly accused of killing a young man. The saint resuscitated the young man and asked him if his father was the culprit. The man answered no before falling back into his eternal sleep. Once his innocent father was freed, Santo António disappeared and regained consciousness in Padua, where he continued his sermon where he had left off.

A LITTLE POEM TO SAINT ANTHONY AS A PROMISE OF LOVE

As Saint Anthony is also the protector of lovers and marriage, in Lisbon, on his feast day (13 June), believers give him a basil plant accompanied by a little poem in which they make a love promise.

Another tradition is that of repairing the jug broken by a young girl, which symbolises both the mending of a ruptured hymen and the virginity of monastic life.

STATUE OF SILENUS, BACCHUS' TUTOR

Museu do Teatro Romano de Lisboa
Pátio do Aljube
• Open Tuesday to Sunday, 10am to 6pm
• Bus: 37

The gods of Roman theatre

Lisbon's Roman theatre, partially excavated on rua de São Mamede ao Caldas and rua da Saudade, was discovered around 1798 when the foundations for buildings in the Baixa Pombalina neighbourhood were dug. Francisco Xavier Fabri, the royal architect of Italian origin, was the first to intervene archaeologically. The excavation and study of this edifice, which is little known by Lisbon residents, continue today.

This Roman theatre of considerable size confirms how important *Olisipo* (the ancient Greek name attributed to Lisbon) already was in this period. The theatre was built in the 1st century, at the time of Emperor Augustus, and reconstructed under Nero in AD 57 by Caius Primus. Partially demolished under the Emperor Constantine, it was finally abandoned in the 4th century and remained buried until 1798.

From 1967 on, it has been the object of several archaeological digs that have succeeded in exposing most of the terracing, the orchestra, the entire stage, and a large number of decorative elements.

Dating from the 1st century, a marble statue of the mythical figure Silenus, the tutor of Bacchus (Dionysus), was discovered there. This suggests that the theatre served to stage orgiastic worshipping rites performed by the bacchanalia and bacchantes who venerated Bacchus, a theory that is supported by the existence of a *vomitorium* (a sort of spittoon in which drunken spectators would vomit).

In addition to this lewd genre of theatre, plays of nobler content were certainly performed, religious pieces for example. During this period, priests also acted and dramatised spiritual myths on stage so as to bring them to the masses and attract the audience to the cults they represented. Located around the theatre were temples of high political and religious importance: the temple of Cybele (near what is now Largo da Madalena), the temple of Thetis (where São Nicolau church now stands), and most important of all, the temple of Jupiter (on which São Miguel d'Alfama church was built).

Yet, at this time when Roman emperors were revered as the gods, the most common genre to be performed at the theatre seems to have been imperial panegyric. It was thus a *Teatro Augustal* whose protector was Emperor Gaius Julius Caesar Octavius Augustus.

THE SYMBOLS OF SAINT LUCIA ⑧

Igreja de Santa Luzia de Malta
Largo de Santa Luzia
• Opening times: 10am to 6pm
• Bus: 37

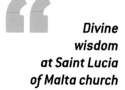

Divine wisdom at Saint Lucia of Malta church

Rebuilt after the earthquake of 1755, *Santa Luzia de Malta* (Saint Lucia of Malta) church bears an azulejo portrait of Saint Lucia on its lateral façade, in addition to two other large azulejo panels representing the conquest of Lisbon and the *praça do Comércio* before the earthquake. Made in the *Fábrica da Viúva Lamego*, they are the work of artist António Quaresma.

Most of the statues once located inside the church have been transferred to the neighbouring São Tiago church, but a few contemporary images of the Order of Malta and the tombs of several noble knights can still be admired.

Many Christian saints are iconographic adaptations of Celtic, Greek and Roman gods for whom Christianity forged sacred legends, thus attributing them with a human existence. Nevertheless, these are fictional stories that only obtain their strength and meaning from the devotion of the people.

Luzia is thus the Christianised equivalent of *Lusina* (*luzia, luz ...*), the Celt-Iberian Sun goddess. She has been kept near the *portas do Sol* (Sun doors) out of respect for the archaic tradition of the sacred enclaves where this saint was, or still is, worshipped.

No study of the martyrs recounts the torture of Saint Lucia, yet it is said that she had her eyes ripped out. She is often depicted carrying her eyes on a platter, thus illustrating the meaning of her name, "she who emits light". Her feast day, 13 December, almost the time of the winter solstice (the birth of light), portrays her as a saint who brings clarity and teaching, like the goddess *Lusina*, the companion of the god *Lug* who sent her to teach her arts to humans. Perhaps this is why the blind invoke her, as in symbolic terms seeing is equated with knowing, and blindness to ignorance.

Thus, the symbolism of *Luzia*, through the luminosity of her name and her attributes (the eyes are sometimes replaced by a lamp or candle), associates her with the ancient goddesses of Wisdom and Light.

This primitive and fortified church, built at the time of Dom Afonso Henriques, thus evokes the presence of the Illuminati of Divine Wisdom who, at the time, belonged to the Order of Saint James of Malta, and who chose Lucia as their Goddess of Light. She bore the same luminous attributes as the Egyptian goddess Isis, she who illuminates and shows the path to perfection.

THE LEGEND OF *SANTA LUZIA* (SAINT LUCIA)

According to legend, Lucia, the virgin of Syracuse (13 December), took her ill mother to the tomb of Saint Agatha in Catania, and, upon her mother's recovery, distributed her belongings to the poor. Denounced to the magistrate Paschasius for being Christian, she was condemned to live in a brothel. She resisted so strongly, however, that even two pairs of yoked oxen failed to move her. She was cruelly tortured. Her eyes were ripped out and, finally, her throat was slit. She thus died a martyr in AD 304. Her attributes are symbolised by two eyes on a platter and, sometimes, by yoked oxen. The legend is thus a reminder that the integrity of the light of religious devotion, sent by God, is such that no mortal man may desecrate it.

PROTECTION FROM FEVER OR SORE THROATS: THE MIRACLES OF SAINT BLAISE

Built in the shape of a Latin cross, Santa Luzia church gives the place of honour to a rare statue of Saint Blaise, a saint reported to be miraculous among Lisbon residents suffering from fevers and sore throats, as well as blind people and those who stutter.

The legend of Saint Blaise (*São Brás*), a Christian bishop martyred by the Romans in Armenia in AD 316, says that he pulled a fishbone out of a child's throat by hand before then placing two lit candles in the shape of a cross on his mouth. This explains why he became the patron saint of throat ailments, as well as the protector of guilds for the professional manufacturers of candles and other wax-based products.

The life-size statue shows Saint Blaise in liturgical robes holding an Episcopal cross. His robe bears the cross of the Order of Malta, of which he was a patron saint (see below), after Saint John the Baptist, the primary protector of this military and religious institution.

According to legend, on 3 February, in the middle of winter, Saint Blaise followed a divine calling and left the city of Sebaste to find refuge in a cave of Mount Argeo, whose etymological root, *arg*, means *argentum* or *argent* (silver). *Arg* is related to *garg*, or *gurg*, which is the root of the word *garganta* (throat). This explains why São Brás became associated not only with throat ailments, but also with caves, thus becoming a representative of the divinities of the profound depths of the Earth.

Saint Blaise is a winter saint whose feast day follows the Feast of the Virgin of the Candlesticks, or Candlemas, on 2 February, almost as if Blaise (*brás* or *braseiro* in Portuguese, meaning "blaze") were the Midnight Sun who, by lighting the candles, would also illuminate the long winter night. In this context, the night signifies the depth, obscurity, and mystery that can only be revealed through the light of the sacred candles. They illuminate this *argent*, the symbolic expression of the pure sacredness of the moon, feminine and intuitive, which is present in this church's *Luz de Luzia*. Saint Blaise is thus not here by chance ...

WHY IS SAINT BLAISE ONE OF THE PATRON SAINTS OF THE ORDER OF MALTA?

Saint Blaise is the exclusive patron saint of the Order of Malta in the city of Lisbon, as the Order of Portugal was apparently founded on his feast day (3 February) during the reign of Dom Afonso Henriques (in the 12th century). Of the 23 command posts that the Order of Malta had in Portugal, Lisbon's was one of the most important, both economically and politically, so much so in fact that Brother Lucas of Santa Catarina, in his memoirs of the military order of Saint John of Malta (1734), enthusiastically describes it as a Grand Priory, which it never was. At the time, the Order's headquarters were located in the Flor da Rosa Monastery at Crato, in Alentejo. The headquarters were set up there in 1340, after leaving Belver or Leça de Bailio at Matosinhos.

THE FORGOTTEN RELIC OF SAINT JAMES MAJOR

⑨

Igreja de São Tiago
Travessa de Santa Luzia, 3
• Opening times: mass at 9am and 6pm
• Bus: 37

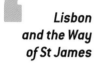

Lisbon and the Way of St James

According to Frei Agostinho de Santa Maria, in the *Santuário Mariano* (a monumental, 20-volume work written between 1707 and 1723), the most precious treasure of São Tiago church was the silver monstrance containing a relic "of the glorious apostle Saint James – Patron of the Spanish Lands" which, every year on 20 January, was carried in the Saint Vincent procession organised by the senate of Lisbon. Today, a bone from the apostle's arm is still there, but now lies in an unidentified wooden reliquary.

The church interior also holds precious Saint James iconography, including two polychrome wooden statues of Saint James the Pilgrim dating from the 18th century. One stands to the left of the main altar and the other in the parish's secretarial offices. On the ceiling of the principal nave, the central painting is original and depicts the Annunciation of the Virgin with Saint James the Pilgrim at her feet. On the first floor of the church, you can also admire an interesting collection of Saint James iconography. The central figure is *Santiago Matamouros* (Saint-James-Kills-the-Moors) at the battle of Clavijo, accompanied by a story of his mysterious apparition. In the church archives, a precious parchment dating from 1 January 1612, Madrid, is secretly preserved. Written by Fray Francisco de Jesus y Xodar, *De la venida del Apostol Santiago a Hespaña* (On the arrival of Saint James the Apostle in Spain) is divided into five *discours* (sermons) that reaffirm the legends that claim the apostle preached in Spain.

Quite early, Lisbon held an important place on the Way of Saint James pilgrimage. The Portuguese route was the main one, leading to Galicia and the apostle's tomb.

Mention of the *Ecllesia Sanctus Jacobus de Ulixbona* (Saint James of Lisbon church) first appeared in 1209 in the Torre do Tombo codex (Portuguese national archives). The church dates from much earlier, however. It became the headquarters of the Knights of the Order of Saint James soon after Dom Afonso Henriques conquered Lisbon on 25 October 1147, and remained so until 1834.

THE MIRACULOUS CROSS OF SAINT JAMES

The miraculous origin of the cross of Saint James goes back to 23 May 844, the date of the battle of Clavijo in Rioja (Spain). This battle took place during the struggle by the Christians to take back the Iberian Peninsula from the Arabs.

The small Christian army led by King Ramiro I of Asturias found itself surrounded in Clavijo Castle on Mount Luterce by the numerous Arab forces led by Abd al-Rahman II. The archbishop of Toledo, Rodrigo Jimenéz de Rada, recounted that Ramiro I saw Saint James Major in a dream, assuring him that he would be present at the battle and that the Christians would be victorious. The next day, the small Christian army left their protective

walls and courageously confronted and defeated the immense Arab forces. The apostle, astride a white horse and brandishing a sword of fire, was seen by all.

Thus led by Saint James *Matamouros* (Kills-the-Moors or Matamore), they vanquished their enemy with a small number of losses.

The apostle's red sword in a cross of fire became the *espatária*, the sword of the military order of Saint James, to whom falls the glory of the Christian reconquest of the Iberian Peninsula.

On the main pediment, you can still see the sculpted coat of arms of the Order of Saint James of the Sword and, above, the date 1773, the year of the church's reconstruction after the earthquake of 1755.

Three military and religious orders took up residence around São Jorge Castle, which was originally called *Apóstolo Santiago e da Santa Cruz* (Apostle Saint James and of the Holy Cross): the Order of the Sword (*Espatários*) at Largo Pequeno de Santiago, at the beginning of Formosa de Santiago street; the Knights Templar, based in Santa Cruz church; and finally the Hospitallers (the future Order of Malta) who occupied the site where Santa Luzia church now stands.

THE MILITARY ORDER OF SANTIAGO

Originally, the military order of Santiago was responsible for protecting and assisting the pilgrims heading to the Cathedral of Santiago de Compostela in Galicia to visit the tomb of Saint James the Apostle. This Saint James Order (*Ordem de Santiago*), which was both military and religious, also played an important role in the fight to take the Iberian territory back from the occupying Moors. The Order was approved by King Ferdinand II of Léon in 1172 and recognised by Pope Alexander III in 1175. The monk-knights first settled in Cáceres, in Extremadura, Spain, but King Afonso VIII of Castile later gave them the town of Uclés. This town became the Order's main headquarters, which is why the early name of the group was the Order of Uclés. The Knights of Saint James, called *Santiaguistas* or *Espatários* (because of their symbol, a cross-shaped sword, or a sword-shaped cross, depending on the point of view – see p. 39), made a vow of poverty and obedience, but followed the law of Saint Augustine, not that of the Cistercians. So they were not obliged to make a vow of chastity and could thus marry (some of the order's founders were married). However, a Papal bull recommended (but did not require) celibacy. The Order's founding statutes followed a principle taken from Paul's Epistles, declaring: "Practising conjugal chastity, living without sin, they follow the model of the first apostolic priests, because it is better to marry than to live under the dominion of one's passions." In Portugal, the Order of Saint James took action from the very beginning of Dom Afonso Henriques' reign, yet it did not draw attention until the reign of Dom Afonso II (1185), becoming well known under the reign of Dom Sancho II (1210). The Order settled in Palmela castle, and then in Alcácer do Sal castle, which became the headquarters of the Portuguese *Provincia Espatária*. This signified the definitive separation of the Portuguese and Spanish branches, as was officialised in 1452 by Papal bull. The great Portuguese knight Paio Peres Correia (1205-1275) was Master Commander of the Order at Alcácer do Sal. In 1242, he was made Grand Master of the Order of Mérida, in recognition of his valiant contribution to the reconquering of Portugal. He had helped to take back a large part of Bas Alentejo and the Algarve from the Moors between 1234 and 1242. It was also thanks to this Order that Dom Afonso III completed the conquest of the Algarve in 1249, by taking the last Moorish bastions in Faro, Loulé, Albufeira and Aljezur. The military Order of Saint James was rewarded with lands in Alentejo and the Algarve. It was given the mission to settle and defend these lands while also developing the paths of pilgrimage leading from Sagres to Lisbon, and on to the final destination – the Cathedral of Santiago de Compostela in Galicia. This explains why many Portuguese villages still hold Santiago Maior (Saint James) as their patron saint today, and why the sword-cross features on their coats of arms. During the reign of Dom Afonso V of Portugal (1448), the order was given a new name – Ordem de Santiago da Espada (Order of Saint James of the Sword). In 1789, Queen Dona Maria I carried out a reform of the military orders. The Great Cross of Saint James of the Sword thus became an honorary order whose Grand Master is the Portuguese head of state.

THE CISTERN OF SAINT MICHAEL OF ALFAMA ❿

Museu do Fado
Largo do Chafariz de Dentro
• Opening times: Tuesday to Sunday, 10am to 6pm
• Guided tour of the cistern by appointment
• Tel: 218823470
• Metro: Santa Apolónia

**Alfama-
the-good-waters**

The waters of *Alfama* or *Águas Orientais* (Oriental waters) were introduced into Lisbon's water distribution system in 1862 through the construction of a cistern and pumping station to replace the former *Chafariz da Praia* (Beach Fountain). The cistern held the water while the steam pumping station propelled it up to the recently constructed Verónica water tower (1868). The *Museu do Fado* (Fado Museum) is located in this cistern, and can be visited by appointment.

The water pumping station's steam machinery has also been preserved in what is now the Fado Museum's auditorium. The enormous cistern is in the courtyard. To access it, you descend a staircase that leads to an underground gallery of arches where the water runs in pipes towards this urban reservoir that was the main water distribution centre for the neighbourhoods around Alfama until the early 1950s.

At the end of the 19th century, these waters, whose temperature sometimes exceeds 20 °C, were classed as mineral and medicinal waters. From the 17th century, they were used for the public baths (*alcaçarias*) that remained in use up to the beginning of the 20th century.

The use of these thermal waters for therapeutic reasons was recognised in the 17th century. Of the two springs that fed the *Alcaçarias do Duque*, for example, the first served to treat skin diseases, digestive problems and allergies, while the second was used for rheumatism, respiratory ailments and women's health problems.

Alfama's main public baths were the *Alcaçarias do Duque* (water temperatures of 30–34 °C), the *Banhos de Dona Clara* (24–28 °C), the *Alcaçarias do Baptista* (32–34 °C) located near São João da Praça at the end of rua do Barão, and the *Banhos do Doutor* (27 °C). After work on the pipes, the spring that used to supply Alfama's *Tanque das Lavadeiras* (Washerwomen's Wash-House) was uncovered. The supposed healing properties of these waters were so reputed that people came from all parts of the country to test them.

The waters, which contain chloride and sulphur but have a low salt content, rise to the surface through a geological fault in the Miocene layers, a fact that you can check on Lisbon Council's geological map. The *Alcaçarias* group structurally originates from five faults roughly oriented north-east to south-west.

THE SECRETS OF CASTELO DE SÃO JORGE ⑪

Rua Santa Cruz do Castelo
• Open daily, 10am to 6pm

> **The castle of 1001 mysteries**

The origins of the Castle of Saint George go back to the dawn of time. Legend says it was a Celtic *castro* (Iron Age fortification), Ulysses' palace and a Sun temple for the Phoenicians, Greeks and Romans. Then came the Mauritanian Moors, before Dom Afonso Henriques, aided by the Crusaders and Knights Templar, took back the city in 1147. The castle then took the name of Santa Cruz, after the fragment of the Holy Cross that the Augustinian monks, companions of Afonso Henriques, had brought back. Upon his marriage to an Englishwoman, Philippa of Lancaster, Dom João (King John I) renamed the castle *São Jorge* (Saint George, the patron saint of England) and made it his royal palace.

Symbolically, the hill on which the castle stood was thus under the aegis of the Holy Cross that indicated the four points of the compass for the establishment of the Roman city.

Dating from the same period as the Christian victory over the Moors, the castle still possesses the medieval door where the martyrdom of Knight Templar Martim Moniz took place. He was crushed to death as he tried to keep the Moors from closing the door so that his fellow knights could enter. The famous legend survived with hardly anyone knowing its true cause. This noble knight had made the Moors and Christians promise not to rampage the city or destroy it, a promise they kept.

If you look closely, you can distinguish unusual signs, emblems and statues here and there throughout the castle. Templar crosses and five-pointed Arab stars (see p. 117) rub shoulders with winged dolphins representing philosophical Perfection and winged lions symbolising spiritual Illumination. The pillars decorated with flaming salamanders fighting one another represent the sacred fire of creation, and the "crow fountain" (*corvo*), bearing the effigy of this black bird in a cage, refers to the darkness and wise secrets of the primitive hermit communities (*carvoarias* or *carvoeiras*) of Islamic Sufism that once lived all along the Lisbon coast.

THE PEREGRINATIONS OF SAINT GEORGE'S STATUE ⑫

Near the castle entrance

> *A statue that paraded through the streets on horseback!*

At the end of the 14th century, in honour of Dom João I of Portugal's marriage to the Duke of Lancaster's daughter Philippa, Saint George (*São Jorge*), the patron saint of England, was chosen to be the patron saint of the Portuguese army.* Lisbon Castle, where the royal palace was located, was also renamed after him.

From then on, the *Corpus Christi* procession, held in June and which regrouped all the patron saints of Lisbon and Portugal, also included Saint George. The procession began at Castelo de São Jorge, where Saint George's statue was attached to a white horse to be led through the city streets under the surveillance of his page and squire, or the "man of iron" who carried Saint George's standard. The squire was generally a cavalry soldier chosen to wear heavy armour and guard the gold and precious stones that decorated the statue's hat and vestments. The domestic servants of the palace helped to transport the saint while trumpets and drums resounded, accompanying the procession. When the cortege arrived at Lisbon Cathedral, a solemn mass was celebrated. The king and the children, accompanied by the nobility and the people, then followed the procession through the streets of Baixa before returning to the cathedral.

Saint George, whose statue now stands at the castle entrance, was replaced in Santa Cruz do Castelo church.

In the 16th century, the worship of Saint George weakened in England as the country became Protestant and renounced the saint. It remained strong in Portugal, however, and, in the 18th century, Dom José I revoked the decree that required the statue of the holy knight to accompany the *Corpus Christi* proces-

sion on horseback. The procession was often difficult, in fact. The page was nearly always injured by the saint himself as the statue, with its lance raised, rocked dangerously back and forth on the horse, often losing its balance and, in a show of utmost ingratitude, injuring the poor page. Today, the saint is placed on a processional litter.

King Dom José I held such devotion for Saint George that his own statue at the centre of Terreiro do Paço could almost be mistaken for that of the saint.

---

*Saint James was the previous patron saint of the Portuguese army.

THE CURIOSITIES OF MENINO DEUS CHURCH ⑬

Igreja do Menino Deus
Calçada do Menino Deus, 15-27
• Visits on reservation through the Patriarchate of Lisbon at 218810500
• Bus: 37; Tram: 12

> ## When Baby Jesus gave Dom João V an heir

Spared by the earthquake of 1755, the astonishing *Igreja do Menino Deus* (Church of the Child God) can only be visited by reservation. At the beginning of the 18th century, a few homes and a chapel that the religious members of São Francisco de Xabregas' Ordem Terceira had acquired to found a hospital stood on this spot. A nun from the *Madre de Deus* (Mother of God) convent offered this new religious edifice a small statue of Baby Jesus. Believed to be miraculous, it was immediately named *Menino Deus* and still exists today.

This name was later extended to the monks' hospital as well as to the new church donated by Dom João V, who had made a vow regarding the long-awaited birth of his first heir. His child's arrival was attributed to the intervention of *Menino Deus* who thus expressed his desire to perpetuate the Lusitanian monarchy, a lineage considered divine ever since Christ had miraculously appeared to Dom Afonso Henriques at Ourique.

Thus, on 4 July 1711, in the presence of the royal family and court, the king laid the first stone of this new church, inaugurating a series of royal building projects that would culminate in the magnificent Mafra convent, the most symbolic Joanina (Rococo style under Dom João V) construction.

The design of this church is attributed to architect João Antunes, and it was his last accomplishment. His plan is original. With the deep apse and unique rectangular nave with cut-off corners, he created a unified, non-

centralised space and the illusion of an enveloping shroud that is accentuated by the arrangement of the lecterns.

The *Igreja do Menino Deus*, whose Mannerist-style façade integrates Baroque elements, is considered to be an architectural model for later Baroque churches whose inspired style strives to humanise the divine, just as Gothicism had earlier deified humanity. Thus, this church inaugurated a new set of ideas for architecture and art, as illustrated in its interior décor, a veritable artistic sampling of Joanina style.

SAINT GENS' CHAIR

Nossa Senhora do Monte and São Gens chapel
Senhora do Monte Belvedere
• Bus: 12

> **Have
> a seat for
> a happy
> childbirth**

The Nossa Senhora do Monte and São Gens chapel is the site of a rather curious tradition. Behind the entrance, in a small cell hidden from the public by a wooden door, is the famous *Saint Gens' chair* (*trono do Santo Jina*), a marble monolith polished into an ergonomic shape by time and the pregnant women who used it.

The legendary character São Gens was, it seems, the seventh Christian bishop of *Olisipo* (Roman Lisbon), soon after AD 300. He was also the disciple of one of the Iberian apostles of Saint James Major, who arrived in the Spanish territory shortly after Christ's Crucifixion. It is said that his mother died giving birth to him. This legend is the origin of a curious tradition in which the pregnant women of Lisbon, hoping for a happy childbirth, come to sit on "Saint Gens' chair". Once located outside the chapel, it is now kept inside. Ordinary women kept alive a tradition that was followed by several queens of

Portugal, such as Catarina (Catherine of Castile), Dom João III's wife and Dom Sebastião's grandmother, who sat on the miraculous "chair".

Four Augustinian hermit monks founded this chapel once Afonso Henriques had taken Lisbon from the Moors. At the beginning of the 13th century, improvements were made by Dona Susana, a noblewoman, as a show of gratitude for her happy childbirth, a fact that contributed to the site's miraculous reputation. It was at this time that the chapel was dedicated to Nossa Senhora da Visitaçao do Monte.

Saint Gens owes his name to the contraction of the Latin *genesius* or *genésio*, meaning *genesis*. The use of the marble chair is thus in perfect accord with the saint's name.

THE STARS OF ESTRELLA D'OURO

Graça district
• Bus: 107

A
"Masonic" district

Located between No. 22 rua da Graça (Grace street) and No. 14 rua da Senhora do Monte (Our Lady of the Mount street), the Estrella d'Ouro (Golden Star) district was designed in 1907 by the architect Manuel Joaquim Norte Júnior. It was built in 1908 on the initiative of Agapito Serra Fernandes, a Galician confectionery manufacturer, to house his workers. Completed in 1909, this "villa", as working-class neighbourhoods used to be called, consisted of 120 households organised into small two- or three-floored buildings built around the Rosalina residence (the owner's home) which stood, isolated, in the centre. Now a retirement home, it is located at No. 13 Josefa Maria street. The gate, which is often left open, leads to a charming collection of homes and gardens, including a beautiful vegetable garden to the left. In an astonishing manner, this neighbourhood is dotted with five-pointed stars. They are on the pavements, the fronts of buildings, everywhere! An important Freemasonry symbol, this star is a reminder of Agapito Serra Fernandes' Masonic membership. He was probably a member of the "Estrella del Noroeste" (Northwest Star) Lodge founded in 1880 in Betanzos (in Galicia's A Coruña province), which was loyal to the United Grand Orient of Lusitania. It is a known fact that architect Norte Júnior was a Grand Orient of Lusitania Freemason who practiced the ancient and accepted Scottish Rite. He even held an important role in the "Amor da Pátria" (Love for the Homeland) Masonic Lodge in Horta, on the Azores archipelago. The layout of the Estrella d'Ouro district is U-shaped and the streets and squares bear the names of members of Agapito Fernandes' family. Take note of the pretty polychrome azulejo panels showing the owner's name, with the star illustrating the district's name (it is sometimes sculpted in relief). The *Ciné Royal* used to be located in this neighbourhood. Inaugurated at the end of 1929, it was the first cinema in Portugal to project films with sound. On

5 April 1930, *White Shadows in the South Seas*, MGM's first film, directed by Van Dyke (who also did the sound), was shown in the presence of the president of the Republic. Now a supermarket (No. 100 rua da Graça), the former cinema's pretty period clock has been preserved.

O NACIMENTO DE CHRISTO

COLÉGIO DOS MENINOS ÓRFÃOS

Rua da Mouraria, 64
- Admission free at any time
- Metro: Martim Moniz

Behind the Mouraria shopping centre, at No. 64 Mouraria street, is the entrance to the *Colégio dos Meninos Órfãos* (School for Orphaned Boys), which is under the invocation of Our Lady of Montserrat. As the door is usually left open, the visit has a certain "semi-forbidden" character that gives it a kind of charm. After crossing a small patio and passing through a majestic Rococo-style gate (from the Dom João V period), you arrive before a veritable marvel of Portuguese azulejo art – a set of 18th-century panels in Rococo frames that stretch all the way up the four floors of the building's staircase. The only one of its kind in Lisbon, it depicts the entire history of the Virgin Mary's ancestors from the House of David, up to the announcement of the Passion of Christ, when as a boy Jesus disappeared from his mother's house and she found him in the Temple among the high priests. This azulejo piece symbolises the former function of the Orphanage School, which was to provide a home to these fatherless and motherless children who were left on their own. They often lived in gangs and roamed aimlessly through Lisbon's streets.

> *A veritable marvel of Portuguese azulejo art*

Queen Dona Beatrice, the wife of Dom Afonso III (Dom Dinis' father), had this home for abandoned children built in 1273. Queen Dona Catherine, the wife of Dom João III, had it renovated in 1549 to welcome more than 30 orphans. She placed it into the good hands of the Society of Jesus, making it the oldest Jesuit orphanage school in the world and transforming it into a unique educational establishment. The building was renovated yet again in 1745 at the request of Dom José I.

After the abolition of the religious orders in 1834, the Colégio dos Meninos Órfãos declined, eventually losing its original function. In the mid-20th century, the building was transformed into a police station (which was later transferred elsewhere), and then into a gym. Conservation work on the building was carried out in 1989 and 1990.

SÃO VICENTE'S ROYAL PANTHEON

São Vicente de Fora Monastery
Largo de São Vicente
• Open Tuesday to Friday, 9am to 4pm; Saturday, 9am to 6pm; Sunday, 9am to 1pm
• Bus: 12

> **A royal pantheon erased from the collective memory since 1910**

Lost in the far reaches of the São Vicente de Fora Monastery, ostracised during the Republican regime that nearly wiped out its memory, the *Panteão Real da 4.ª Dinastia de Bragança* (Royal Pantheon of the 4th dynasty of Bragança) was founded by Dom João IV, who, in his will, clearly expressed his desire to build sumptuous mausoleums here for himself and his descendants.

The tombs, placed in the church at first, were transferred to the former refectory of this monastery of Augustinian monks in the 19th century. It was King Dom Ferdinand I who decided to have this pantheon remodelled in order to regroup other royal tombs dispersed throughout various religious buildings.

Most of the tombs take the form of large marble mortuary drawers on each side of the large hall. Embellished above with crowns, the names and titles of their occupants are engraved in gold on the front. Here, one can find the tombs of Dom João IV, Dom Carlos I and queen Dona Amelia, crown prince Dom Luís Filipe and the last king of Portugal, Dom Manuel II. A few members of the Bragança family are missing. Dona Maria I rests in the Estrela Basilica, Dom Pedro IV in the do Ipiranga monument at São Paulo, and Dona Maria Pia in the Superga basilica in Turin.

The Pantheon's current form dates from 1933. On the anniversary of the regicide, a private commission of monarchists asked architect Raul Lino to create a double tomb to hold the mortal remains of Dom Carlos and Dom Luís Filipe. Reminiscent of a medieval double tomb and simultaneously inspired by the tomb of Dom João IV, these tombs were placed in the centre of the hall. At their head stands the statue of a woman representing grief, the work of sculptor Francisco Franco. Some believe she resembles Dona Amelia, the widow queen and mother, crying with her face buried in her hands, and who thus also symbolises the country crying for its martyrs assassinated in the Republican attack of 1908, at Terreiro do Paço.

BAIXA - ROSSIO

BAIXA POMBALINA'S SACRED ARCHITECTURE

Covering an area of 23.5 hectares, the Baixa Pombalina district came into being after the earthquake of 1755 through the efforts of the marquis of Pombal (see p. 209), the Minister of Public Works of King Dom José I. His drafts show a square-shaped network that was built by two corporations: the *Casa dos 24* (House of 24), founded in 1383, and the *Casa Real dos Maçons da Lusitânia* (Royal House of the Builders of Lusitania), founded in 1733.

In 1716, under Dom João V, Lisbon had already been divided into two parts: east and west. Following hermetic tradition (see below), the marquis of Pombal also kept the city's 12 pre-existing neighbourhoods (which were thus numerically equal to the 12 signs of the zodiac) reflected by the 7 hills representing the 7 traditional planets. He also planned 17 large avenues, thus using the number 17, which is a key number for Portugal (see p. 102).

Three main avenues lead from *Terreiro do Paço* (Palace terrace), *rua Augusta* (in the centre), *rua do Ouro* and *rua da Prata* (on either side). They symbolise the caduceus representing Mercury, which is composed of a central column around which two snakes, one black and one white, intertwine; one snake is solar (golden) and the other lunar (silver). These serpents (*ofiússas*) represent the arteries through which vital

energy flows. The lunar artery is cold and passive, while the solar one is hot and active. In traditional symbolism, gold represents the Sun and silver the Moon. *Rua do Ouro* (Gold street) thus corresponds to the caduceus' solar aspect, while *rua da Prata* (Silver street) corresponds to its lunar aspect. As for *rua Augusta*, it symbolises the central column, the channel that fuses and synthesises the two polar forces.

HERMETISM: REFLECTING THE ORGANISATION OF THE COSMOS ON EARTH TO ATTRACT CELESTIAL ENERGY

As described in the works of Hermes Trismegistus (which were long considered to be Egyptian), the hermetic tradition believes that reproducing the organisation of the heavens (stars, planets, etc.) on Earth (in the design of a city or the ceiling of a room, for example) is a way of attracting divine energy to the place in question.

THE SEVEN SACRED HILLS OF LISBON

According to one of the popular legends about the origins of Lisbon, the city was founded by Ulysses who fell in love with Ofiússa, the queen of the snake-women. When Homer's hero returned to his Greek homeland aboard the *Argos*, thus abandoning Ofiússa, she was so furious that she made the plateau of Ulisibona (or Olisipo), now Lisbon, tremble. From her rattles sprang the seven hills of the city.

The tradition, a blend of myth and prophecy popular with Lisbon residents, declares that the seven hills of Lisbon refer to the seven gates of Heavenly Jerusalem, as represented by Lisbon's seven principal Christian temples which stand at the top of each hill: São Cristóvão, São Vicente de Fora e Sé Velha, São José da Anunciada, Nossa Senhora da Graça, Chagas de Cristo, Santa Catarina, and São Roque.

The idea of transferring the sacred meaning of the seven hills of Jerusalem (Gared, Goath, Acra, Bezetha, Moriah, Ophel and Zion) and of Rome (Campidoglio, Quirinale, Viminale, Esquilino, Celio, Aventino and Palatino) to Lisbon, coinciding with the Sun's course from east to west, is a very ancient one. However, it took on an elaborate form in the works of 17th-century Portuguese authors such as Frei Nicolau de Oliveira, who superimposed Lisbon's greatness on that of Rome.

The capital's seven hills (an allegory of the seven elements of matter: atomic particles, subatomic particles, ether, air, fire, water, earth) are: São Jorge in Mouraria; São Vicente in Alfama; Santa Ana in Anunciada; Santo André in Graça; Chagas in Carmo; Santa Catarina next to Largo de Camões; and São Roque in Bairro Alto.

The Tagus river flows at the foot of the seven hills. According to the sacred tradition, it thus symbolises the river of Paradise (*Paradhesa*) that bathes the seven spiritual poles (Qutbs or Chakras in Arab and Sanskrit) that bring life to the seven primordial lands (Aqtabs or Dwipas, in Arab and Sanskrit).

HERMES TRISMEGISTUS AND HERMETISM: ATTRACTING CELESTIAL ENERGY TO EARTH BY REPRODUCING THE COSMIC ORDER

Hermes Trismegistus, which in Latin means "thrice-great Hermes", is the name given by the neo-Platonists, alchemists, and hermetists to the Egyptian god *Thot*, *Hermes* to the Greeks. In the Old Testament, he is also identified with the patriarch Enoch. In their respective cultures, all three were considered to be the creators of phonetic writing, theurgical magic, and messianic prophetism.

Thot was connected to the lunar cycles whose phases expressed the harmony of the universe. Egyptian writings refer to him as "twice great" because he was the god of the Word and of Wisdom. In the syncretic atmosphere of the Roman Empire, the epithet of the Egyptian god *Thot* was given to the Greek god *Hermes*, but this time was "thrice great" (*trismegistus*) for the Word, Wisdom and his duty as Messenger of all the gods of Elysium or Olympus. The Romans associated him with *Mercury*, the planet that mediates between the Earth and the Sun, which is a function that Kabbalistic Jews called *Metraton* (see p. 181), the "perpendicular measure between the Earth and the Sun".

In Hellenic Egypt, *Hermes* was the "scribe and messenger of the gods" and was believed to be the author of a collection of sacred texts, called *hermetic*, that contained teachings about art, science, religion and philosophy – the *Corpus Hermeticum* – the objective of which was the deification of humanity through knowledge of God. These texts, which were probably written by a group belonging to the *Hermetic School* of ancient Egypt, thus express the knowledge accumulated over time by attributing it to the god of Wisdom, who is in all points similar to the Hindu god *Ganesh*.

The *Corpus Hermeticum*, which probably dates from the 1st to the 3rd centuries AD, represented the source of inspiration of hermetic and neo-Platonic thought during the Renaissance. Even though Swiss scholar Casaubon had apparently proved the contrary in the 17th century, people continued to believe that the text dated back to Egyptian antiquity

before Moses and that it announced the coming of Christianity.

According to Clement of Alexandria, it contained 42 books divided into six volumes. The first treated the education of priests; the second, the rites of the temple; the third, geology, geography, botany and agriculture; the fourth, astronomy and astrology, mathematics and architecture; the fifth contained hymns to the glory of the gods and a guide of political action for kings; the sixth was a medical text.

It is generally believed that Hermes Trismegistus invented a card game full of esoteric symbols, of which the first 22 were made of blades of gold and the 56 others of blades of silver – the *tarot* or "Book of Thot". Hermes is also attributed with writing the *Book of the Dead* or "Book of the Exit towards the Light," as well as the famous alchemy text *The Emerald Table*, works that had a strong influence on the alchemy and magic practised in medieval Europe.

In medieval Europe, especially between the 5th and 14th centuries, hermetism was also a School of Hermeneutics that interpreted certain poems of antiquity and various enigmatic myths and works of art as allegorical treaties of alchemy or hermetic science. For this reason, the term *hermetism* still designates the esoteric nature of a text, work, word or action, in that they possess an occult meaning that requires a hermeneutic, or in other words a philosophical science, to correctly interpret the hidden meaning of the object of study.

Hermetic principles were adopted and applied by the Roman *Colegium Fabrorum*, associations of the architects of civil, military and religious constructions. This knowledge was transmitted in the 12th century to the Christian *Builder-Monks*, the builders of the grand Roman and Gothic edifices of Europe, who executed their work according to the principles of sacred architecture, true to the model of sacred geometry. It is the direct legacy of volumes three and four of the *Corpus Hermeticum*, according to which cities and buildings were constructed in interrelation with specific planets and constellations, so that the design of the Heavens could be reproduced on Earth, thus favouring cosmic or sidereal energies. All of this was done with the purpose of achieving the hermetic principle that states: "Everything above is like everything below".

During the European Renaissance (16th and 17th centuries), hermetism was replaced by humanism. Forms were rationalised and the transcendental ignored. It was the end of the traditional society and the beginning of a profane, Baroque and pre-modernist society, paving the way for the arrival of the materialism and atheism that dominates the modern world. There were, however, some exceptions to this predominant rule in Europe. In Portugal, in the 16th century, the *Master Builders*, the heirs of the Builder-Monks, founded the Manueline style (see p. 174) according to the hermetic rules of sacred architecture. The influence of the *Free Builders* continued into the 18th century and their greatest work was the restoration of Lisbon after the earthquake of 1755. That is why Pombal's Lisbon is designed and constructed according to the geometric and architectural measures of the Tradition handed down by Hermes Trismegistus.

THE MYSTERIOUS CAIS DAS COLUNAS ❶

• Metro: Terreiro do Paço

> **The Masonic entrance for the future "emperor of the world"?**

The *cais das Colunas* (quay of the Columns) got its name from two monolithic pillars that stand at each end of the *Praça do Comércio* (Market square), designed by architect Eugénio dos Santos during the city's reconstruction after the earthquake of 1755.

These biblically inspired and clearly Masonic columns are identical to the *Jakim* (Wisdom) and *Bohaz* (Devotion) columns of Solomon's Temple. The *cais das Colunas* opens onto the Tagus and its Atlantic estuary, beyond which lie other continents, civilisations and cultures. It is thus the world's gateway to Lisbon, which is why, quite early on, the Sebastianists believed that the "Secret King" (also called the emperor of the world or the "Desired One" – see p. 134) would eventually disembark here, arriving from the "Island of Utopia". The Royal House of the Freemasons of Lusitania probably used the myth to have Masonic columns placed on the quay. Right across from the quay, an equestrian statue of Dom José I stands in the middle of the square facing the quay, ready to announce the arrival of the universal emperor. Behind him, the Augusta street arch opens Lisbon to the world. The underlying concept of the architectural and artistic design of the entire Praça do Comércio is to personalise the divine attributes of the last *sephiroth* (sphere) of the Judaeo-Christian Kabbalah's Tree of Life (see p. 181), *Malkuth*, the symbol of "Reign" and the "World." The cais das Colunas thus becomes the entrance to the "Temple of the Desired One" that the square represents; the Augusta street arch is the gate to the "City of Mysteries".

No written document has been found that mentions the year the cais das Colunas was built. All that is known is that it was completed at the end of the 18th century because it features in a colour engraving by Noel and

Wells entitled *A view of the Praça do Comércio at Lisbon*, dating from 1792. The columns collapsed at the end of the 19th century and were not replaced until 1929. Dismantled in early 1997 for works related to the extension of the metro between Chiado and Santa Apolónia, the cais das Colunas regained its rightful place on the Terreiro do Paço or Praça do Comércio on 25 August 2008.

THE SYMBOLS OF THE EQUESTRIAN STATUE ❷ OF KING DOM JOSÉ I

Praça do Comércio
• Metro: Terreiro do Paço

> *Praça do Comércio and Mafra convent, at the heart of theories about the Fifth Empire?*

At the centre of Terreiro do Paço stands the equestrian statue of King Dom José I (1714-1777) designed by Machado de Castro and cast by Bartolomeu da Costa, and which was inaugurated on the king's birthday (6 June 1775). The statue's location was imposed by Eugénio dos Santos' design. It occupies the geometric centre of an equilateral triangle whose corners point to the Augusta street arch and the lateral gates of the two large towers that complement the square's openness. It is interesting to note that, when you superimpose the layout of Mafra convent on that of Terreiro do Paço, the apse and the statue of the Lusitanian emperor stand at exactly the same spot, and the convent's two large towers are at the same latitude as those of the square.

Some people have concluded that the proportions of the two locations are equal and complementary, their intention being to situate the temporal capital of the world here, and the spiritual capital seven leagues away at Mafra, in accordance with the conception of the inspired ideology of the Fifth Lusitanian Empire (see p. 70). This *translatio imperii* theme is also present in the remarkable bas-relief on the back of the statue's base. Here, the crowned Child, near his mother, receives Lisbon's coat of arms from defeated Rome. At his feet lies a treasure-filled chest that a dignitary is offering him, while an architect shows the design of New Lisbon to the Virgin Mary.

At the top of the monument, Dom José I, dressed in "Roman style" with a cape of the Order of Christ and holding the imperial sceptre, sits astride a horse that is crushing serpents (*ofiússas*), an iconic symbol of *São Jorge*, to whom the monarch was devoted. Here, he takes on the role of God's king-priest (see p. 70) who, it is said, will govern the Fifth Empire of the World from Lisbon, which explains why his face is turned towards the Tagus estuary and why he looks towards distant continents.

Below, on the sides, *Triumph* (horse) and *Renown* (elephant) symbolise the West and the East. The *Renown* of the East (the ancient era) transfers its true values to the *Triumph* of the West (the new era). The trumpeter angel near the elephant and the angel holding a palm leaf near the horse dominate the old man, who represents the profane. They symbolise the spiritual traditions of the East and West uniting in Lisbon.

THE SYMBOLS
OF LISBON'S TRIUMPHAL ARCH

❸

• Metro: Terreiro do Paço

> **Did the Rosicrucians inspire the layout of Lisbon and Washington DC?**

Although many European cities possess a triumphal arch representing the Temporal Empire, Lisbon's arch represents, above all, the idea of the Spiritual Empire. Indeed, it appears to have been built so that, one day, the Secret Universal Emperor may pass through it, thus inaugurating a New Age for the world in Lisbon, according to the Fifth Empire tradition. From this mythic and sacred point of view, this triumphal arch thus represents the symbolic, final door towards humanity's last *translatio imperii* (see p. 70).

Symbolically, the arch evokes the threshold of mysteries, and the doorway from the shadows of ignorance to the Light of Wisdom that mythical Lisbon conceals. It announces the spiritual Resurrection, as signalled by the Saint Andrew's cross with, at its centre, the secret king's rose, which can be seen at the interior crown of the arch. The arch's rear façade, on the Augusta street side, displays an enormous clock that fatally marks the time until the coming of the Fifth Empire.

The rose and Saint Andrew's cross indicate that the Free Builders of the marquis of Pombal period, who rebuilt New Lisbon after the earthquake of 1755, were inspired by the mysticism of the ancient Rosicrucians, followers of primitive Christianity. The Rosicrucians appeared in Portugal in 1700, first hidden by the Franciscan piety of the Espírito Santo de Mafra convent where they resided, then revealed in 1717, by the Casa Real dos Maçons Lusitanos (Royal House of the Lusitanian Freemasons). No sooner had Lisbon been rebuilt than these mystic followers disappeared from Portuguese history books. Some say then went to establish the city of Washington DC in the United States, whose layout is largely inspired by that of Lisbon.

The triumphal arch of Augusta street is a monumental accomplishment, on the scale of Pombal-period architecture. It was not entered in an architectural competition until 1843, under the Costa Cabral government, and not built until 1862. It was finally completed in 1873, thanks to a project by Veríssimo José da Costa and the intervention of Vítor Bastos and the Frenchman A.C. Camels.

Camels' sculpture, which tops the monument, represents Glorious Lusitania, shown as the Great Universal Mother, rewarding Apollo and Minerva (Inspiration and Understanding) or, in another interpretation, "Glory crowing Genius and Valour".

THE TRANSFER OF POWER – TRANSLATIO IMPERII

The Latin expression *translatio imperii*, which means both "succession of empires" and "transfer of power", is a concept created in Europe in the Middle Ages to describe history as a linear phenomenon – a succession of transfers of power from a supreme governing power, or *imperador*, to the next, who controls the *imperio*, and which is marked by well-defined cycles.

Generally, authors described the *translatio imperii* as a succession that resulted in placing the supreme power in the hands of the king or emperor who ruled the region in which they lived. They established the spiritual and temporal origin of their country leading to the solid establishment of imperial power by incorporating former cultures that had contributed to the development of the country's religious, cultural and social characteristics. Some notable examples are:

Otto de Freising (who lived in what is now Germany, from 1114 to 1158): Rome – Byzantium – the Francs – the Lombards – the Germans (the *Holy Roman Germanic Empire*);

Chrétien de Troyes (who lived in medieval France, from 1135 to 1190): Greece – Rome – France (the *Frankish Empire*);

Richard de Bury (England, 1287-1345): Athens – Rome – Paris – London (the *Franco-Breton Empire*).

The authors of the Middle Ages and the Renaissance legitimated

this transfer of power through a relationship between a royal figure and a god or hero of Greek or Roman antiquity, as Virgil had done when he made Aeneas (a Trojan hero) the mythical founder of the city of Rome in the *Aeneid*. Following the same tradition, in the 12th century, the Anglo-Norman authors Geoffrey of Monmouth (in his *Historia Regnum Britanniae*) and Wace (in *Brut*) attributed the founding of Great Britain to the arrival of *Brutus* of Troy, the son of *Aeneas*. In the same manner, the French Renaissance writer, Jean Lemaire de Belges (in his *Illustrations of Gaul and the Singularities of Troy*), connected the founding of Celtic Gaul to the arrival of the Trojan, *Francus*, son of *Hector*, and that of Celtic Germany to the arrival of *Bavo*, *Priam*'s cousin. Thus, an illustrious genealogy was established for *Pepin* and *Charlemagne* (the legend of *Francus* was the basis for Ronsard's epic poem *La Franciade*). The erudite origin of the Lusitanian *translatio imperii* lies in the works of the Cistercian Joachim of Fiore (see p. 188), born in Calabria (Italy) around 1132. In his work

Liber Figurarum, he divides the world into three universal ages: that of the Father, the Son and the Holy Spirit. The first is situated in the past in Jerusalem, the second in the present in Rome, and the third in the future in Lisbon. Joachim of Fiore drew his inspiration from the Old Testament texts of the prophet Daniel in which Daniel interprets the dream of a statue of King Nebuchadnezzar as an early vision of Paradise on Earth.

Several writers have justified Portugal's particular mission by referring to the following verse from the scriptures: "For so hath the Lord commanded us, saying, I have set thee to be a light of the Gentiles, that thou shouldest be for salvation unto the ends of the earth" (Acts 13:47).

An astute expert on the subject, Luís de Camões (1525-1580) also prophesied about Lisbon a little later, in *Os Lusíadas* (The Lusiads), VI, 7 (from the 1776 translation by William Julius Mickle, published in 1877):

"Resolv'd in Lisbon glorious to renew
The Roman honours – raging with despair
From high Olympus' brow he cleaves the air,
On earth new hopes of vengeance to devise,
And sue that aid denied him in the skies."

Using the same principle, the idea of transferring the sacred meaning of the seven hills of Jerusalem and Rome to Lisbon (see p. 61), following the path of the sun from east to west, also took on an elaborate form among the Portuguese authors of the 17th century, such as Frei Nicolau de Oliveira who superimposed the grandeur of Lisbon on that of Rome.

Finally, Joachim of Fiore's three ages of the world concept was reformulated by Father António Vieira (1608-1697) (see p. 72) who wrote of five ages, the last being the Fifth Portuguese Empire, the future spiritual and temporal Fifth Empire of Humanity of which Lisbon would be the birthplace. The preceding empires were the Assyrian, Persian, Greek and Roman; the

Portuguese empire will be the last. The first empire (Assyrian) was ruled by the Father; the second (Persian) by the Father and the Son; the third (Greek) by the Son; the fourth (Roman) by the Son and the Holy Spirit; the fifth (Lusitanian) will be ruled by the Holy Spirit, symbolised by the "return of Dom Sebastian" (see p. 105), a simple allegorical representation of the true king and priest of God, Christ, who will have Lusitania ("Land of Light") for the *Parousie* (presence/return of the Lord).

Absolutely identical to the Egyptian obelisk of Rome's Piazza Navona fountain, das Necessidades obelisk-fountain, on Largo do Rilvas, is a clear reference to the principle of the *translatio imperii* from Rome to Lisbon, which, according to myth, was to occur sometime after 2005 during the astrological era of Aquarius and would inaugurate a new period of progress for humanity.

FATHER ANTÓNIO VIEIRA AND THE FIFTH EMPIRE

Father António Vieira was born to a family of humble origins on rua do Cónego, near Sé Cathedral (a commemorative plaque has been placed next to the front door of the house) in Lisbon on 6 February 1608. He was the eldest of the four children of Cristovão Vieira Ravasco, originally from Alentejo (his mother was the daughter of an African/European mulatto woman), and Maria de Azevedo, a Lisbon native. Cristovão served in the Portuguese navy and was a clerk for the Inquisition for two years. He left for Brazil, alone, in 1609, to fill the clerk's position at Salvador da Bahia; his family later joined him.

António Vieira arrived in Bahia at the age of six and began his schooling at Salvador's Jesuit school. A rather disastrous student at first, "thanks to the intervention of Our Lady", he became the most brilliant. Legend says that one day when he skipped school, an angel appeared to him to show him the way back. In May 1623, when he had just entered the Society of Jesus as a novice and was having great difficulty acquiring the required knowledge, he prayed, crying, to the Virgin Mary, asking her to inspire him. He felt a shock and fainted. When he regained consciousness, he found himself gifted with a remarkable intelligence that made him a striking figure of his time.

Indeed, António Vieira was the most influential person of the 17th century in Portugal and Brazil. A monk of rare spirituality, an inspired writer and passionate orator, he was also a great humanist defender of the rights of the oppressed. In politics, he distinguished himself as a missionary in Brazil where he tirelessly defended the rights of the indigenous people, fighting against their exploitation and enslavement. In return, they gave him the name Paiaçu (meaning "Grand Father" in the Tupi language).

Following his humanist code of ethics in Portugal, António Vieira also defended the Jews, the abolition of the distinction between New Christians (converted Jews, persecuted by the Inquisition) and old Christians (traditional Catholics), and the abolition of slavery. In fact, he strongly criticised the priests of his period and the Inquisition.

He was an early follower of the ideal of Sebastianism and again entered into conflict with the Inquisition, which accused him of heresy based on a 1659 letter in which he explained his theory of the Fifth Empire and Portugal's future supremacy in this great future empire to the Bishop of Japan. He was thrown out of Lisbon, banished and imprisoned in Porto, then in Coimbra. In 1667, he was condemned to imprisonment and was prohibited from preaching, but six months later the sentence was annulled.

He returned to Brazil in 1681 and there compiled his writings in order to publish the 16 volumes of his *Sermons* and to complete the *Clavis Prophetarum*, the key of the prophecies exposed throughout his works, and notably in his *História do futuro* (*History of the Future*), a work in which he presents the five Ages of the World, Lusitania being the dominating element of the final age. He published more than 500 letters in three volumes.

In literature, his *Sermons* are considered to be of capital importance for the Portuguese and Brazilian Baroque period. They are often assigned reading at university.

In 1694, elderly and feeble, he was no longer able to write. On 10 June, his last suffering began and he lost his voice. He died on 18 July 1697, aged 89, at the Jesuit School in Salvador da Bahia.

PORTUGAL: THE "HEAD" OF THE "BODY" OF EUROPE?

The fact that Europe is sometimes seen as a *Body* comes from a 14th-century map (1335-37) by Opicinius de Canestris; three different versions of the map are known today. Later, Sebastian Münster, the Franciscan of Basel, published a map in his work *Cosmography* that was largely inspired by this medieval map. His colleague and fellow countryman, Heinrich Bünting, published it, with a few additions, in his main work *Itinerarium Sacrae Scripturae*, and again in his work *Pro Hispaniae Defensio* with the corrections of Portuguese humanist Damião de Góis. In the 17th century (1624), Julião de Castro, in his *History of the Goths*, makes Europe a woman of whom Spain is the head and Portugal, her crown. This provoked, in 1631, the following comment by António de Souza Macedo in his *Flores de España, Excelencias de Portugal*: "which is honoured in Portugal, because if there are heads that honour certain crowns, in general it is the crown that honours the head."

In this notion, taken up by Fernando Pessoa in his poem *O dos castelos* (The Castles) from the book *Mensagem* (Message), and by Camões in Song III, verses 17 and 20 of *Os Lusíadas*, the Iberian Peninsula is thus the *head* of Europe and the Italian peninsula (which is boot-shaped) is its feet. The head, or the coordinator, and the feet almost touch while the *arms* are thrown back, as if ready to jump into the waters of the Atlantic; the Portuguese "face" fixedly stares at the American horizon. Each country corresponds to one of the other organs.

54 Das ander Buch

Although all the ancient versions of maps unanimously place Portugal at the head of Europe, they sometimes differ in the placement of some countries, even if the commonly held positions are the following: the *feet* and the *legs* are in the Italian peninsula while the *genital region* is in the Balkans. The *base of the spine* is also positioned there and is thus connected to Eastern Europe, the zone from which creative energy (called *Kundalinî* in the East) emanates. Austria-Hungary is the *solar plexus*, the *navel* region, and the *intestines*, and is also connected to the East. The *lungs* are linked to Switzerland and Central Europe, the zone of fiduciary circulation (money, capital) that makes the entire trade sector function. The *heart* is in France and Luxembourg (the word *Luxembourg*, like *Lusitania*, means "place of light" – it is from Luxembourg that the founders of the Portucalense earldom came, this place where all the doctrines blend harmoniously). The *arms* are in the industrial zone of Northern Europe (Germany, the Low Countries, Britain and Scandinavia), which represents the working Europe. The *head* is the zone that stretches from the Pyrenees to the extreme west of the Iberian Peninsula, Portugal (and Galicia) representing the crowned *face* and the *forehead* of all Europe. It may therefore be concluded that Portugal mentally and spiritually drives Europe, which, for the greatest harmony for everything and everyone, should encourage Culture, the *spirit* of Portugal.

Note also that, in the body, the brain dominates the inferior organs, even if they obviously also have the power to affect it, and that, when the brain dies, the entire body dies along with it.

FERNANDO PESSOA'S TABLE

Martinho da Arcada café-restaurant
• Metro: Terreiro do Paço

> *Where Pessoa dreamed of the "Fifth Empire"*

The *Martinho da Arcada* café-restaurant will always be linked with one of its regular customers, *Fernando Pessoa*, who wrote most of his poems there, including those of the only book he published during his lifetime – *Mensagem*.

In a quiet corner, enjoying a cup of coffee, a glass of brandy and a cigarette, he evoked Bandarra and António Vieira, dreamt of a secret king and a Fifth Empire, and tried to reveal and announce Portugal's greatest destiny with certitude (see p. 70).

To honour the greatest contemporary defender of the Portuguese language, the manager of *Martinho da Arcada* has left the table and chair where the poet habitually sat. Photographs and autographs of the author surround it. Today, it is the inevitable meeting place for the literary gatherings of Pessoa specialists and admirers. Some of them, and more than just a few, are so immersed in their passion that they have adopted the poet's mannerisms.

Located in one of the corners of Terreiro do Paço under the arches that gave it its name, this café-restaurant has been in existence since 1778. First known as the *Café da Neve* (Snow Café), it was located in one of the first buildings erected on the Praça do Comércio after the earthquake of 1755. It served various drinks and was known at the time for its ice cream, which explained its name, *Café da Neve*. Then, in 1784, it changed its name to the *Casa de Café Italiana* (Home of Italian Coffee) because of its Italian owner, Domingos Mignani, before then becoming *O Café do Comércio* in 1795. Around 1809, it was commonly called the *Café dos Jacobinos* because many Jacobins and libertarians of the period passed time there. In 1820, as the *Casa da Neve*, it was owned by a man called Simão Fernandes, and welcomed Lisbon's high society who came to enjoy its still popular ice cream. In 1823, the restaurant changed its name and owner, a certain Anselmo, yet again, before being bought just a year later by José de Melo. In 1829, yet another new owner, Martinho Bartolomeu Rodrigues, arrived and gave the establishment its current name. He carried out extensive refurbishment that transformed the place into one of the best café-restaurants in Lisbon. In his last will and testament, he bequeathed it to the clerk of the Commercial Court, Julião Bartolomeu Rodrigues, who thus became its owner in 1899.

FERNANDO PESSOA:
"IF YOU ARE A FREEMASON, I AM MORE – I AM A TEMPLAR."

There is no clear evidence proving that poet and essayist Fernando António Nogueira Pessoa (Lisbon, 13 June 1888 – Lisbon, 30 November 1935) was, in fact, a Freemason, even if nowadays many factions of this institution claim to be the poet-prophet's followers.

Fernando Pessoa had an early interest in occultism and even frequented this milieu between 1910 and 1920, driven by the desire to know more about the mysteries of life. This was how he came into contact with spiritualism and theosophy in 1912 and began translating English theosophical books into Portuguese in 1915. An astrology buff, he set himself up as an astrologer in Lisbon in January 1916, under the pseudonym Rafael Baldaya, completing more than a thousand horoscopes. During this period, he kept up a regular correspondence with the famous English occultist, Aleister Crowley, who came to visit him in Lisbon on 2 September 1930.

Pessoa's insatiable thirst for knowledge, together with his great familiarity with occultism, led him to develop his thinking based on the notion of spiritual "Portugueseness", linked to the coming of the Fifth Empire (see p. 70).

At the time of António Salazar's rise to power and the establishment of the *Estado Novo* in 1933, Fernando Pessoa quickly declared himself against Salazar, especially when his essays and poems began to be censored. He then wrote a series of anti-Salazar poems. Salazar, a fan of ancient Roman dictatorships, decided to abolish all the Initiatory Orders and spiritual movements in Portugal. When deputy José Cabral's bill prohibiting secret associations and, notably, Portuguese Freemasonry, was presented before Parliament, Fernando Pessoa publicly opposed it in a brilliant article published in the *Diário de Lisboa* on 4 February 1935.

In defence of the religious freedom and *Traditional Spirit* that characterised Freemasonry, he declared, "I am not a Freemason and I belong to no other order, similar or not. Yet I am not anti-Freemasonry either, for what I do know about it persuades me to be fully in favour of it."

Because of this article, Fernando Pessoa remains connected to Freemasonry. There are even lodges that bear his name, despite the fact that he was never a member. He was simply a fervent defender of the freedom of expression and of religious worship, whether it be Freemasonry or some other leaning.

Finally, in his work "Identity Card", written in Lisbon on 30 March 1935, Fernando Pessoa openly revealed his position on spirituality.

"Religious opinion: Christian gnostic and consequently opposed to all organised churches, and especially the Church of Rome. Loyal to the secret tradition of Christianity that is intimately linked to the secret tradition of Israel (the Holy Kabbalah) and to the occult spirit of Freemasonry.

Initiatory position: initiated, directly from Master to Disciple, in the three inferior degrees of the Knights Templar of Portugal (apparently abolished)."

At last, as Fernando Pessoa summed up in his poem *São João* (9 June 1935), "If you are a Freemason, I am more – I am a Templar".

Pessoa e "O caminho da serpente"

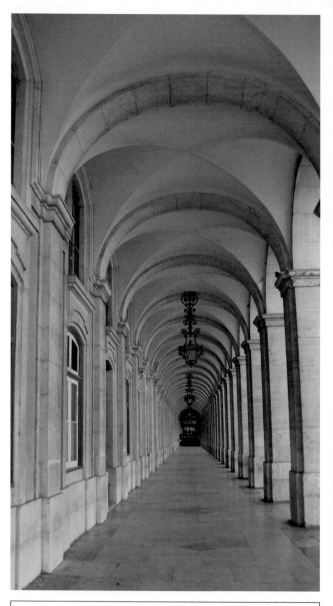

The tarot is also sometimes referred to as the "Book of Thot". *Thot*, the Egyptian god of wisdom, who is known as *Ganesh* by the Hindus and *Hermes* by others, is considered to be the originator of this card game.

❺

THE HIDDEN MESSAGE
OF THE MARKET SQUARE

Praço do Comércio
• Metro: Terreiro do Paço

> *Tarot*
> *behind*
> *the design of*
> *the Market square*

In the aftermath of the 1755 Lisbon earthquake, the entire region around the Tagus was destroyed and the contours of a new *Praça do Comércio* (Market square) were carved out on the former *Terreiro do Paço* (Palace terrace). The achievement of architects Eugénio dos Santos and Carlos Mardel, this square has become the hallmark of the Pombaline period.

The fruit of Carlos Mardel and the marquis of Pombal's knowledge of esoteric and Masonic ideals (Pombal was closely linked to the Freemasonry of Vienna, Austria), the former square was largely conceived in reference to the tarot card game.

A tarot deck consists of 78 cards or blades, the first 22 of which are golden or esoteric (the 'major arcana' or trump cards), and the other 56 silver or exoteric (the 'minor arcana' or pip cards).

The buildings on each side of the square each have 28 arches, making a total of 56, like the 56 pip cards. On the main façade, between *do Ouro* (Gold) and *da Prata* (Silver) street, there are 22 arches, 11 in each direction beginning at Augusta street, like the 22 trump cards.

As the two sides of Augusta street have 22 arches, the monumental triumphal arch is thus the 23rd, the first 'minor arcanum'. It is also the gate leading to the village of Mafra, seven leagues away, where the *Convento do Divino Espírito Santo* (Convent of the Divine Holy Spirit) was initially conceived as a Heavenly Jerusalem, of which the Terreiro do Paço was its earthly home. The site thus ultimately symbolises the message of Heavenly Jerusalem that will descend on Lisbon, the chosen city (see p. 70).

Note the dolphin heads, a symbol of the *philosopher's stone*, at the top of each arch on the square.

THE UNDERGROUND THERMAL BATHS OF RUA DA PRATA

6

Rua da Conceição No. 77
• Open 26 to 28 September
• Admission free

> **Thermal baths only open to the public three days a year**

Every year, for three days in September, the underground galleries of rua da Prata are open to the public. The entrance is on rua da Conceição, next to No. 77. Entry is prohibited the rest of the year because the galleries are usually flooded and water must be pumped out to open them to visitors.

This site was not discovered until 1771 during the neighbourhood's reconstruction after the earthquake of 1755. The solid structure had survived the terrible catastrophe.

Known as the "Roman thermae" of rua da Prata, this network of underground galleries used to serve as the foundation to a street-level construction. Its robust vaults are characteristic of the Roman constructions found on unstable land, used to support the edifices above.

The discovery of an octagonal-shaped system with a roof of decreasing height, a stele invoking Asclepius (god of medicine), and a water reservoir quickly led to the conclusion that these were, indeed, thermal baths. Even though the site possesses vestiges of construction from the Ibero-Punic era (the time of Emperor Tiberius), it seems to date from the first half of the 1st century AD (reign of emperors Julius and Claudius).

The stele to the god Asclepius may have been brought from the thermal baths of Cassius, near rua das Pedras Negras, even if the therapeutic qualities of Lisbon's underground waters were celebrated in both places from the time of Julius Caesar. Indeed, Caesar had granted the city the status of *Municipium* and, in recognition of this fact, had given it the name *Felicitas Julia*.

LISBON – LIX BONA – GOOD WATER?

According to Father Agostinho Veloso, the name *Lisboa* comes from the root *lix* meaning "thermal water" that is slightly cloudy, as if it had been mixed with ashes. In fact, *lix* or *lixa*, as the Romans later pronounced it, in Latin (like the Celtic root *li*) means *acqua cinere mixta*.
The Romans added the Latin adjective *bona* to create the word *lixbona* or *luxbona*, which survived in popular language and meant "good water".

THE BLAZING EAGLE OF SÃO NICOLAU

Corner of Augusta and São Nicolau streets

> **A symbol of the city's rebirth after the 1755 earthquake**

At the corner of Augusta and São Nicolau streets, people often walk by without noticing the uncommon silhouette of an eagle among flames. The high relief is most likely the work of sculptor Joaquim Machado de Castro or his assistant, Francisco Leal Garcia, as they were the sculptors of the reconstruction of the Baixa Pombalina district after the 1755 earthquake. Like the mythical phoenix rising from its ashes, the eagle of Lisbon (in antiquity, Portugal was represented by an eagle, which was also the imperial emblem of Lisbon) rose from the destructive fires caused by the terrible earthquake of 1755.

THE EAGLE: THE ONLY BIRD WITH DOUBLE EYELIDS CAPABLE OF STARING DIRECTLY AT THE SUN

For the Greeks and Persians, the eagle, which is capable of staring directly at the Sun, was linked to the *Sun* and *Jupiter*. The Egyptians called the eagle *Ah* and dedicated it to the god *Horus*, and by extension *Osiris*, while the Copts venerated it under the name of *Aham*. For the Greeks, the eagle was the sacred emblem of *Zeus*, and for the Druids, it represented the *Supreme God*. Medieval bestiaries compared the eagle with *Adam*, the Father of Humanity, because, in the beginning, he lived near God. This symbol has survived to modern times thanks to the crowned heads of Europe. Following the example of the Roman general Marius (who made the two-headed eagle the emblem of the imperial Rome in the 2nd century BC), they chose this king of the air to represent their families. The two-headed eagle was also the emblem of the royal families of Russia, Poland, Austria and Germany. Jupiter, however, was satisfied with a one-headed eagle, as was the blazing Sun. Such is also the case for the eagle on Augusta street, which symbolises the indivisible unity of the Spirit of Christ whose ascension is sometimes illustrated by an eagle. The eagle flies at high altitudes and looks directly at the Sun, just like the Son before God the Eternal Father.

ROSSIO CINEMA'S ART NOUVEAU FAÇADE **8**

Rua dos Sapateiros No. 229

> *A vestige of the first "luminous projections using Drumont's light"*

The *animatógrafo do Rossio* (Rossio cinematograph) is the last survivor of the grand epic of the birth of cinema in Portugal.

Located on rua dos Sapateiros (Cobbler street), near the Arco do Bandeira (Flag Arch) that opens on to Praça do Rossio, this *cinematograph* opened on 8 December 1907. With more than 100 seats, this theatre in the city centre was first known as the *Rossio Palace*. In addition to serving as a cinema, it was also a children's theatre. The stage, like all the interior decor, is in Art Nouveau style, with balustrades and small forged iron gates separating the stage from the orchestra pit.

It is said that the children's theatre company, "Tim-Tim por Tim-Tim", sponsored by Baron Henrique Álvaro Antunes da Silva Neves, eventually

disbanded in Lisbon after a final performance here at *Rossio Palace*. The company had even travelled to perform in São Salvador da Bahia, Brazil, where it had achieved great success at the Teatro São João at the turn of the 20th century.

Now a pornographic cinema, the building has preserved a few traces of its past splendour and greatness on its main façade. The Art Nouveau decor and two polychrome azulejo panels, signed "M. Queriol, 1907" and made in collaboration with Jorge Pinto in his Ajuda workshop, are especially noteworthy.

The first "luminous projections using Drumont's light" – the first film projections – took place in Lisbon on 10 December 1894, on the second floor of the Chiado Department Stores, which had opened their doors a few weeks before.

SYMBOLISM OF THE STATUE OF DOM PEDRO IV

9

Praça do Rossio

Four figures that protect Portugal at the centre of Lisbon

Inaugurated on 29 April 1870, the monumental column of Dom Pedro IV, in the centre of Praça do Rossio, displays a group of unusual statues at its base.

Placed at the four corners of the monument's pedestal (itself bordered with the coats of arms of important Portuguese cities) and dressed in Graeco-Roman ceremonial gowns, the figures represent the four suits of a deck of cards – clubs, spades, diamonds and hearts – which, respectively, are the popular symbols of the Episcopal cross (*paus* in Portuguese means both "trefoil" and "sticks" or "clubs"), the royal sword (*espadas* in Portuguese means both "spade" and "swords"), the protective star (*ouros* in Portuguese means both "diamond" and "gold") and the Eucharist cup (*copas* in Portuguese means both "heart" and "cups"), which are the magical attributes of the four angels of destiny that Easterners called *Devas Lipikas*. The arrangement of the figures at the corners suggests that they protect the whole of Portugal from this *mundus* (see opposite page), this point of axis that is Lisbon, its capital.

In the Kabbalistic Judaeo-Christian tradition, these figures are iconologically known as the four crowned angels (archangels) whose traditional names are Raphael, Michael, Uriel and Gabriel.

The statue of *Prudence*, who holds a round shield marked with a serpent in her right hand and represents the suit of diamonds, faces the direction of Rossio central station, where the statue of Dom Sebastião stands.

Temperance, who holds a cup (the suit of hearts), looks in the direction of the Santo António gate, and, through this hermit of the desert, becomes a symbol of the sacerdotal art.

Leaning against a club (the suit of clubs), *Force* contemplates the Carmelite convent where the holy warrior Nuno Alvares Pereira lived.

With her sword (the suit of spades) and characteristic scales, *Justice* turns towards Lisbon's Sé Patriarcal cathedral.

At the top of the monument, *Power*, personified by emperor Dom Pedro IV, looks toward the triumphal arch of Augusta street and the *cais das Colunas* (quay of the Columns) (see p. 65), which, symbolically, is where the Secret King, Portugal's and the world's last hope, will disembark and take the place of Christ on the altar of the Universal Fifth Empire (see p. 70).

A circle of *tágides* (Tagus nymphs) lies above these figures, adding grace and depth to the monument and serving as a protective circle around this "totem pole".

> The statue also illustrates an archaic and mythic symbolism related to the celestial battles between the archangels Michael and Samuel, here personified by Dom Miguel I and Dom Pedro. These two royal brothers and rivals for the throne provoked the Portuguese Civil War (1828-1834).

AXIS MUNDIS

The *world axis* (also called the *cosmic axis, centre of the world, world pillar* or *columna cerului*) is an omnipresent symbol that crosses human cultures. The image, which is a reflection of the macrocosm in the microcosm, expresses a central point of connection between the Heavens and the Earth from which the four cardinal directions radiate. This central point functions like an *omphalo* (navel) or the primordial centre of an urban centre, a pole from which everything radiates but which is also the meeting point of the north-south (*cardo*) and east-west (*decumanus*) axes.

The task of imagining the area between Rossio and Terreiro do Paço, rebaptised *Baixa Pombalina*, was entrusted to Hungarian architect Carlos Mardel (Poszony, Hungary, 1696 – Lisbon, 1763). This *perfect quadrilateral* forms a network made up of seven lateral streets and seven longitudinal streets. To achieve this result, Mardel began with the Rossio, the starting point for all directions, thus following the Roman architectural tradition of the *mundus* or *axis mundi*, the "fundamental axis" created from the crossing of the vertical *cardo* (which, here, starts at the beginning of Terreiro do Paço) and the horizontal *decumanus* (which, here, connects Braço de Prata to Costa do Sol).

At the centre of Praça do Rossio stands a monumental column, appearing like a phallus, a Hindu *linga* or a Latin *mundus*. At its summit stands the statue of Dom Pedro IV holding the *Carta constitucional* (Constitutional Charter) of 29 May 1826 in his right hand. This monument was created by sculptor Elias Robert and architect Gabriel Davioud, both of whom were French.

THE MEDALLION OF TWO JOINED HANDS

Corner of rua do Amparo
• Metro: Rossio

> *Fraternal union between two squares*

A few metres from Praça do Rossio and Praça da Figueira (Fig Tree square), at the corner of rua do Amparo (Mutual Aid street), a rather discreet medallion on the side of the building depicts two joined hands. A typical Masonic symbol, here it signifies the mutual aid between two squares.

This high relief was probably designed by Freemason architect Carlos Mardel who built Praça do Rossio and made it the central and vital pole of the city by moving the rural market that was once held there to the nearby Praça da Figueira. It was here that the main market was set up in 1755 after the ruins of the Todos os Santos hospital, which had burned down in 1750 and then collapsed in the earthquake, were cleared. This central market, which is now installed in an enclosed space in Art Nouveau style, had several successive names: *Horta do hospital* (Hospital vegetable garden), *Praça das Ervas* (Herbs square), *Praça Nova* (New square). In 1849, a wrought-iron fence with eight gates was installed around the already covered market. The square thus became one of the emblems of Pombaline Lisbon, thanks to its remarkable construction for the period and its importance as the true supply centre of the Baixa district.

Da Figueira, Rossio and Comércio squares became the three principle poles of the city's activities. The political or ministerial sector formed around Praça do Comércio, making it the centre of the country's political life, while the commercial or urban sector was centred on Rossio, with its countless shops and offices. And finally, rural life was focused on Figueira central market.

Thus, the two hands that join in a fraternal fashion unite Baixa's two squares and, through their traditional symbolism, express the union between the countryside and the city.

THE MASONIC SALUTE

Freemasons salute each other by shaking hands in a distinctive manner. By pressing with their thumb, they indicate their rank. Using the tip of the thumb of the right hand, an apprentice will lightly touch the first knuckle of the other person's right index finger three times: two rapid touches and one long one. A companion will do the same, but will use his right thumb to touch the first knuckle of the other person's middle finger five times: two rapid touches, a long one, and two more rapid ones. A master will do likewise, but with seven touches: four rapid ones and three long ones.

THE DOLLS' HOSPITAL

Praça da Figueira, No. 7
• Admission free

> **The oldest dolls' hospital in Europe**

At No. 7 Praça da Figueira, in the centre of Lisbon's Baixa district, the *Hospital das Bonecas* (Dolls' Hospital) has been in business since 1830. Europe's oldest dolls' hospital, it is rather unique, as the dolls' hospitals of Madrid and London only repair valuable dolls, and that of New York is much more recent and provides fewer services. For almost 180 years, this hospital has continued to piece together the dreams of young children, the recollections of those who are no longer so young, and the memory of the past for all.

When dreams need repair, little ones, their parents and grandparents turn to the *Hospital das Bonecas*, through whose doors pass all sorts of sick or damaged dolls that sadden the imaginary world of their owners, especially children. All of them are treated with great care, from the old cardboard dolls made in Portugal until the 1960s, to Barbie dolls and McDonald's Happy Meal figurines.

The system of admission and treatment of the dolls is the same as in any hospital. When a patient arrives, his owner goes to the reception desk and fills out a form with a bed number that allows the hospital to identify the patients. Then, the dolls are placed on a stretcher, called *tinoni*, and are taken up the stairs to the workshop on the next floor. Each room is named according to the treatment provided. First, there is the plastic surgery room, where dolls are restored, repainted and given a new hairstyle. The trauma room is next door; it is for dolls that were the victims of games that were far too violent for their constitution. At the end of the hall you will find the transplant room full of legs, arms and heads of all styles and sizes, and next to this room is the morgue, where the doll doctors sometimes go to retrieve transplant parts. Finally, the residents' room is for dolls abandoned by their owners ...

When dolls become so damaged that they can no longer be fixed, their parts are donated to artists or, as has already been the case, to the *Hospital da Estefânia*, a specialised children's hospital that has been known to make paediatric prostheses from doll parts.

PAINTING OF BOCAGE'S ARREST

Café Nicola
Praça do Rossio
• Open 9am to 11pm

Inside *Café Nicola*, one of the oldest literary cafés in town (it was mentioned in the *Gazeta de Lisboa* as early as 1787), a huge painting that dominates the room depicts a rather comical and memorable incident involving Bocage, the poet.

> **"I'm Bocage, I've come from Café Nicola and I'll be in the next world if you fire that pistol"**

A billiard room was once connected to the café by a long corridor. Its entrance was at what is now Nos. 22 and 23 Praça do Rossio. This is the spot where Bocage was stopped by one of the chief of police Pina Manique's men who, aiming his pistol, asked: who are you, where have you come from, and where are you going? Bocage supposedly answered with a quatrain that has become famous, "*Eu sou o Bocage, venho do café Nicola e vou para o outro mundo se disparas a pistola*" ("I'm Bocage, I've come from Café Nicola and I'll be in the next world if you fire that pistol"). Was he under surveillance for his supposed Freemason membership, under the pseudonym *Lucrécio*, from 1795 to 1797? Whatever the case, the incident was immortalised in the painting by Fernando Santos, who is also the artist responsible for the café's other paintings. Undoubtedly the primary representative of the "Arcádia Lusitana" literary movement that he founded and popularised, Manuel Maria de Barbosa l'Hedois du Bocage (1765-1805) was a regular of *Café Nicola*. This is where he cursed his enemy, ex-priest Agostinho de Macedo, dictated his *Pena de Talião* (a satire about the latter) to a friend, and also where Nuno Pato Moniz wrote the comic poem *Agostinheida*, in which he ridiculed the famous priest for his dissolute lifestyle.

Bocage also recited improvised sonnets here, drawing a plethora of intellectuals and politicians. Even after the poet's death, his group of friends continued to meet at the café and organise literary gatherings. José Pedro da Silva, one of the café's waiters who had befriended the poets, helped them as best he could, notably by lending them enough money to make ends meet. He was even the person who paid for Bocage's burial.

Café Nicola closed in 1834 and did not reopen until 2 October 1929, when it adopted Bocage as its mascot. The façade, which also dates from 1929, was completed by Norte Júnior. Although the interior decor was originally neoclassic in style, architect Raul Tojal changed it to Art Deco style in 1935.

Café Nicola also has a statue of Bocage sculpted by Marcelino Norte d'Almeida.

IGREJA DE SÃO DOMINGOS

Largo de São Domingos
• Metro: Rossio

A murky history that weighs the church down?

São Domingos church is the largest in Lisbon. Major religious ceremonies, state and royal funerals, as well as royal baptisms and coronations are held here. Although it was founded during the period of Dom Afonso III (1242), it was greatly

modified under Dom Manuel I. Annexed to the Dominican convent and the tribunal of the Holy Office in the 16th century, this church quickly became synonymous with terror, not only for Lisbon's Jews, but also for all those who came into conflict with the all-powerful superiority of the Church. This was where the Dominican Inquisition held its *autos-da-fé*, condemning poor, unfortunate souls who had dared stand up to the Church to be burned alive at the stake in Terreiro do Paço.

THE INQUISITION AT SÃO DOMINGOS

São Domingos Church is linked to the historic *São Domingos massacre*, on 19 April 1506, when thousands of Jews and New Christians were massacred by the populace roused to a fury by the monks, more because they coveted their possessions than for religious reasons. During the celebration of the mass, a monk pointed out a powerful ray of light illuminating the cross and interrupted the worship with his hysterical shouts of "Miracle! Miracle!" A New Christian objected, saying it was a simple reflection. The furious monks incited the population's fury that spread throughout Lisbon in a horrible massacre that spared no one, not the elderly, nor the sick, nor the children. More than 2,000 people were killed.

In the earthquake of 1755, the church was strongly shaken and was the first of all the Inquisition's courts to fully collapse. It was rebuilt, but on the night of 13 August 1959, a violent fire entirely destroyed the interior, as if the church's own murky past weighed on its very existence.

EL REI

D. JOÂO IV

INDEPENDENCIA

THE PANELS OF THE RESTORATION

Gardens of the palace of the Counts of Almada
- Guided tour by reservation
- Tel: 21 324 14 70
- Largo de São Domingos
- Metro: Rossio

The forgotten azulejos of the Independence

Located at the centre of Lisbon's Baixa quarter, near Praça do Rossio and São Domingos church, the Palace of the Restoration is known by several names: *Palácio des Condes de Almada* (Palace of the Counts of Almada), *da Restauração* (of the Restoration), or *da Independência* (of the Independence). When the patriotic revolt of 1 December 1640 took place, the palace's owner, Dom Antão de Almada, reunited here the 40 conspirators that gave Portugal back its independence after 60 years of Castilian rule. The conspirators met in secret in the palace gardens, which Dom Fernando de Almada, a captain of the Portuguese army, and his wife had bought from nobleman Dom Nuno de Barbudo in the 15th century. Upon entering the gardens, two large, cone-shaped brick towers can be seen on the roof (similar to the conical chimneys of the royal palace in Sintra) that Dom Antão de Almada had built and which illustrate the typical style of the Restoration period. Hardly touched by the earthquake of 1755 and relatively unknown to most Lisbon residents, the azulejo works called the *Panels of the Restoration* are located in the palace gardens. Dating from 1696, they are the work of Gabriel del Barco. One of them depicts the conspirators meeting here, in the gardens, as the title indicates: *Blessed place, honourable meetings where Portugal's Redemption was fulfilled.* Other panels show the victorious attack against the Spanish regents at the palace of Ribeira and the triumphal procession celebrating the Restoration.

In the garden, against the *fernandina* wall (from the period of King Dom Fernando in the 14th century) and to the right of the fountain and azulejo panels, lies another room where the conspirators' secret meetings were supposedly held. The participants descended the staircase in the *fernandina* wall, knocked on the door below, and, as a sort of password needed to gain entrance to the pavilion, showed a small silver tube that had a hidden spring at one end. Once activated, an image of Nossa Senhora da Conceição, the protector of Portugal, would appear.

WHEN CHRIST DETACHED HIS RIGHT ARM FROM THE CROSS TO BLESS LIBERATED PORTUGAL

The fountain in the centre of the garden shows an angel below the words, "*Redemption of Portugal, Fidelity and Love triumph.*" This fountain represents the *Angel of Portugal Restored*, a theme based on the pious and patriotic legend that recounts that, during the procession celebrating the nation's independence, the Christ at the top of the crucifix held by Father Nicolau da Maia supposedly detached his right arm from the cross to bless the population and thus all of newly liberated Portugal.

THE SECRETS OF
THE DOM SEBASTIÃO STATUE

Rossio station
Largo Dom João da Câmara

15

> *17,*
> *Portugal's key*
> *number*

At the centre of Rossio station's main façade, at the point where two horseshoe-shaped arches meet, stands a statue of Dom Sebastião, the king who perished in the battle of *Alcazarquivir* (Arabic *Ksar el-Kebir*, Battle of the Three Kings) in North Africa, 1578.

As Rossio central is a place of waiting and of hope, there is no better place for this departed king who determined Portugal's fatal destiny. As a result of his defeat, the country fell under the rule of Castile, thus losing its independence for 60 years.

The number 17 can be found everywhere on this façade. The king is shown at the young age of 17. He is dressed in period clothing, bears his royal insignia on his chest, and holds a shield sporting Portugal's coat of arms in front of him at an angle of 17°. Note that 17 is also the total sum of the façade's eight doors and nine windows. In addition, the number 17 refers to Portugal's "biorhythm" as its history seems to unfold in 17-year cycles (see p. 102). The king holds his sword in front of his shield; his hands seem to hide two castles, leaving five visible, a symbolic reference to the Fifth Empire tradition elaborated in Lisbon and imagined at Sintra (see p. 70). In the façade's two horseshoe-shaped arches, one can also see the horseshoes of the white horse on which the Secret King is supposed to arrive one misty morning, as prophesised by the Portuguese Sebastianic utopia – a prophesy with which the statue's sculptor, Simões de Almeida, was probably familiar. Almeida had already sculpted a plaster model of Dom Sebastião when he was crown prince (1874), a work he later created in marble, in 1878, and which figured in the Paris World's Fair.

This building's exuberant neo-Manueline style exterior was designed by architect José Luís Monteiro in partnership with Adães Bermudes. Built in 1886-87, the station was opened on 23 November 1890 and was called the *Estação Avenida*. It was an audacious accomplishment for the period, since it applied an architectural style and aesthetic movement that had only been used for royal, noble or other official edifices to a public railway station.

On 14 December 1918, another king-president, Sidónio Pais, was assassinated at the foot of this statue. At the time, many people acclaimed Pais as a reincarnation of Dom Sebastião. Perhaps it was for that reason that he was assassinated.

17, PORTUGAL'S KEY NUMBER

Several authors justify Portugal's special mission by referring to the following verse from the Bible: "I have set thee to be a light [*Lux*] of the Gentiles [*Citânia*], that thou shouldest be for salvation unto the ends of the earth" (Acts 13:47). They also refer to the salutary role of the arcanum 17 in tarot – *Hope*, a card that bears the name *Star*. The miracle of the battle of Ourique (25 July 1139, Saint James Day, according to the Chronicle of the Goths) seems to have confirmed this mission. During the famous battle, Christ supposedly appeared to Dom Afonso Henriques and assured him that he would renew the Portuguese nation in the sixteenth generation to follow him (which corresponds to Dom Sebastião). We should note that sixteen generations, plus the original generation, makes 17 generations.

In tarot, the number 17 is the *Star*, which indicates "that which is secret must be revealed", in accordance with the etymological meaning of the term *Apocalypse*. Furthermore, adding the 1 and the 7 of 17 gives the number 8, which, in tarot, corresponds to the card of *Justice*, represented by the Archangel Michael, and which is adapted from the celebrated saying "you are born in Portugal either with a mission or as a punishment". In other words, those born in Portugal either serve humanity or suffer with it, meaning that the two extremes are one and the same. In his horoscope of Portugal, Fernando Pessoa (see p. 78) begins with the year 1128 (24 June, the date of the battle of São Mamede between Dom Afonso Henriques and his mother Dona Teresa) and ends with 1978. It is interesting to note that the period covered is 850 years, or exactly 50 cycles of 17 years. From 1877 to 1978, Portugal would go through a lunar (punishment) cycle, with the period after 1978 marking the beginning of a new global solar cycle that would create the conditions necessary for Portugal to carry out its world

mission in full. Astrologically, Pessoa links Portugal's entrance into the "Fifth House of the Sun" to the five wounds of Christ (which themselves are related to the five shields on the Portuguese flag) and to the idea of the Fifth Empire (see p. 70) ruling over the entire world from Lisbon.

The number 17 is also the exact number of streets in the Baixa Pombalina district, as well as the number of figures depicted in the central panel of Nuno Gonçalves' polyptych (see p. 150). Nor should we forget the national standard, which used to be displayed at an inclination of 17° to the right and was not set upright until the reign of Dom João II. You can see the coat of arms displayed in its original form on the statue of Dom Sebastião at the entrance to Rossio central station (see preceding page).

WHY WAS PORTUGAL'S COAT OF ARMS STRAIGHTENED?

Dom João II (1455-1495), thirteenth king of Portugal, was nicknamed the *Perfect Prince* for his authoritarian and Machiavellian exercise of power. During his reign, he took constant reprisals against the nobility who opposed his absolutism. He suppressed the municipal councils and dispossessed the Order of Christ, the main force of resistance, and even went so far as to have his administrator, Dom Diogo, duke of Viseu, assassinated in 1484. The duke was stabbed in the back in the palace of Setubal.

In 1485, the king ordered that all the insignias of the Order of Christ be removed from the caravels. He had already had those of the House of Avis eliminated and replaced by royal emblems identifying no specific group, thus considerably weakening the national spirit. Understanding nothing of the symbolism of the Portuguese coat of arms, Dom João II had the shields of Portugal's armorial bearings modified with the so-called "Operation to straighten the coat of arms" carried out in the same year. To the nobility who tried to oppose the change, he responded with the famous phrase, "I am the lord of lords, not the serf of serfs".

DOM SEBASTIÃO, THE "CHIMERICAL KING"

Dom Sebastião I (Lisbon, 20 January 1554 – Alcazarquivir, Morocco, 4 August 1578) was the sixteenth king of Portugal and the seventh of the Avis dynasty. He was the son of Prince Dom João, who himself was the son of Dom João III and Dona Joana, the daughter of Holy Roman emperor Charles V. Dom Sebastião left no descendants. Dom Sebastião became heir to the throne at the death of his father, two weeks before his birth. He became king in 1557, at the age of three. The long-awaited heir of the Avis dynasty, he was known as *The Desired One*, *The Hidden One*, or *The Dormant King* (a sort of *Messiah*) because of the legend telling of his return one misty morning to save the nation (see "Sebastianism", p. 134).

Dom Sebastião's tutor, Jesuit father Luís Gonçalves da Câmara, made of him a visionary monk, while his riding instructor, Dom Aleixo de Menezes, turned him into a passionate horseman. These two threads to his education, particularly the first, made of Dom Sebastião an accomplished military monk, a Roman Catholic who fanatically opposed heresy and a man exalted at the idea that Portugal would dominate the world. The stage was set for the tragedy that would ruin the country.

The chivalric ideal conceived by Dom Sebastião pushed him to devour the works of this literary genre, to turn over the tombs of his ancestors at the monastery of Batalha in search of who knows what, in his frenzied desire for military feats surpassing those of previous kings. His religious ideal made of him a Puritan, a feigned ascetic who dreamed of running through the Sintra mountains and finding a "Grail".

At the age of 14, Dom Sebastião took over the governing of the Empire. Of fragile health and simple of mind, he dreamed only of battles, conquests and spreading the Faith. Consecrating little time to the affairs of his vast empire, he was profoundly convinced that he would be Christ's captain in a crusade against the Moors of North Africa and would conquer Jerusalem, where he would become "King of the World" (see p. 152). Dominated by his dreams of glory, he ignored the sensible advice of his wisest councillors and, in his madness, went off to lose himself, and Portugal along with him, in the midst of the African sands of Ksar el-Kebir (Alcazarquivir). He was 24 years old. The unfortunate young king's uncle, Filipe II of Spain, occupied Portugal, politically and militarily subjugating it to Castilian rule; the nation's independence was lost. Soon, patriotic hopes that the lost Dom Sebastião would return to deliver the country from its Spanish occupiers arose, thus giving rise to the Sebastianist myth of *The Hidden One* (see p. 134).

To put an end to the development of Sebastianism, Filipe II had the supposed body of the lost king transported to the monastery of the Hieronymites in 1581, but this did not help in the least as there was no proof that it was indeed the lost king. And yet, engraved on the tomb were the words, "Dom Sebastião, king of Portugal and of everything else", meaning the world.

O PALÁCIO DE
SANTOS O VELHO
NO SÉCULO XVI

D. Sebastião: o Encoberto

LIMA DE FREITAS' FIFTH EMPIRE PANELS ⑯

Rossio station
Largo Dom João da Câmara

I n Rossio Station, 14 polychrome azulejo wall-panels are exhibited near the platforms. Produced by the *Fábrica de Cerâmica de Constância* in 1995-96 and based on models by Lima de Freitas (Setúbal, 1927 – Lisbon, 1998), these wall-panels are inspired by the myths and legends of Lisbon.

"Portugal has a lot to teach and bring to Europe"

Initially influenced by neo-realism, Lima de Freitas quickly dedicated his work to the Portuguese imagery he drew and painted so skilfully, rather in the manner of Almada Negreiros, to whom he was close. His murals filled with symbols notably depict the theories of the Fifth Empire (see p. 70), as the panel entitled *Vieira and the V Empire* so clearly illustrates.

The immense knowledge contained in these panels led Gilbert Durand, a personal friend of the artist, to declare, "Portugal itself has many more myths

than all of Europe put together, which could perhaps help the latter realise its destiny."

The following words from Lima de Freitas seem to echo Durand: "Portugal has no reason to feel ashamed with regard to the rest of Europe. On the contrary, we have a lot to teach and bring to it. The Mission that concerns our principal qualities – our deeply-rooted sense of human brotherhood, the idea of Universality, and the vision of the Fifth Empire."

A fifteenth panel by the same artist can be seen in the Restauradores metro station, which is directly connected to the central station.

SECRET PASSAGES OF THE AVENIDA PALACE ⑰ HOTEL

Rua Primeiro de Dezembro, 123
• Metro: Restauradores

*Spies
at Avenida Palace*

Although Portugal remained neutral during the Second World War, the *Avenida Palace* hotel was a nest of German, British and American spies. The hotel's oldest employees tell incredible stories about this period and show interested visitors some of the secret passages used by the spies. The hotel was so notorious for this reason that Lisbon is even mentioned in the film *Casablanca*.

On the fourth floor, a mysterious door leading to another door that has been locked since 1955 can still be seen. Behind it, a corridor connects the hotel to Rossio station, which allowed VIPs and spies arriving under diplomatic cover to arrive incognito and evade police controls.

One legendary spy was known by the code name *Garbo*. A Spanish citizen living in Lisbon, this spy gave the Germans false information fabricated from simple geography books about the British way of life. Thanks to him, the Germans came to believe that they had lost the aerial war with Britain, although that was not necessarily the case. This all happened in the period before the Allied invasion of Europe when rumours circulated about the possible landing sites: Normandy or the Pas-de-Calais, which was the more likely option given its proximity to Britain.

Considered to be the most luxurious hotel of the Baixa district, the *Avenida Palace* was founded on 10 October 1892 by the *Wagons-lits* tourism company, based in Paris. Architect Luís Monteiro was in charge of the project aimed at European tourists arriving in Lisbon at Rossio station. The hotel has 85 rooms and 11 suites, a large lounge, a *Belle Époque* restaurant and an Empire-style dining room. The hotel's illustrious guests have included Emperor Hirohito of Japan, who spent his honeymoon here, banker Alves dos Reis, admiral Américo Thomaz and the Portuguese president Sidónio Pais, who was assassinated on his way to the hotel.

THE UNDERGROUND ABBEY OF PALÁCIO FOZ ⑱

Palácio Foz
Praça dos Restauradores
• Visits by appointment. Tel: 21 322 12 15 or 21 322 13 62

A secret underground abbey

Still today, an extraordinary "abbey", a former restaurant where secret meetings were held up to the 1940s, lies beneath the Palácio Foz. It is closed to the public but can be visited by appointment.

It is divided into three sections: the *claustrum* (cloister) with its *taverna vínica* (wine tavern) as the distich indicates, the *refectorium* (refectory) inspired by the Roman Cistercian cloisters of the Iberian Peninsula, and the *coro* (choir) that overhangs the refectory and leads to the *cells*. This restaurant was almost exclusively reserved for the Masonic elite (men and women of the Ancient and Accepted Scottish Rite of Freemasonry) as well as for the elite members of the Club dos Makavenkos, a bohemian society that organised banquets and whose members, for the most part, were connected to Masonic humanism. The site is entirely based on esoteric symbolism (Masonic, Kabbalistic and theosophic) and is inspired by Lusitanian myths. The Masonic presence cannot be denied as 24 small busts of Freemasons, both men and women, some of whom bear the insignia of their rank on their chest, line the *refectorium*'s north and south walls. Also seen there is a strange, mythic figure (a dragon-woman), doves and swallows in relief in the corners of the room, ship rudders bearing the effigies of Vasco da Gama and Pedro Álvares Cabral, the hanging statue of a medieval architect, a beautiful coral fountain next to a well leading to underground Lisbon, and a small balcony decorated with ropes, pulleys and a fisherman's knot, underneath, in relief. Red marble Tuscan columns and green marble colonnades further enliven this place reserved for the secret meetings and *agapes* (see page 112) of Lisbon's Freemasons.

The Palácio Foz, which was the largest residence in Lisbon until the end of the 19th century, was owned by the marquis of Castelo Melhor who had it built in 1777, following a design by Italian architect Francisco Xavier Fabri. Later, in 1889, the Castelo Melhor family sold the palace to financier Tristão Guedes de Queirós Correia Castelo Branco, the second count and first marquis of Foz.

In April 1917, the *pastelaria Foz* (Foz pastry shop), which occupied several rooms on the ground floor as well as the cellar, opened its doors. In the cellar, an Art Nouveau restaurant, the *Abadia* (Abbey), was launched in a blend of neo-Gothic and neo-Manueline styles.

FREEMASON *AGAPES*

Modern Freemasonry inherited the *agapes* (also called *banquets*) tradition, which was popularised in Portugal during the Napoleonic wars, from the Judaeo-Christian tradition. In their purest sense, the *agapes* are Popular Feasts of the Empire of the Divine Holy Spirit, where everyone, regardless of social class, shared the same table for the *bodo* (meal), after the mass. Of Portuguese origin, these feasts were celebrated in Alfama and São Sebastião da Pedreira.

Agapes is Greek for *love feast*. The early Christians celebrated this feast as illustrations of friendship, love and mutual benevolence. These charity banquets were begun in Rome by Saint Clement during the reign of Domitian (1st century) and come from a tradition directly inherited from the Mysteries of the Sun god Mitra that Christianity adapted in the episode of the Last Supper of Jesus Christ (see our guide *Secret Rome*).

The early Christians celebrated these fraternal banquets before they celebrated Eucharistic communion. Composed of various dishes, and not simply bread and wine, they were presided over by apostles, then later by bishops and priests. From the 3rd century, the *agapes* had a tendency to degenerate into orgies, to the point that the Church abolished them when

a bishop could no longer control them.

In the 18th century, the Masonic tradition reclaimed the hierarchical organisation and traditions of early Christianity, including the ritual *agapes*, which are directly connected to the meals or *banquets* of Masonic lodges. Nevertheless, the *santo beijo* (holy kiss) and women were excluded from them, and the banquets became more like "drinking" feasts than "love" feasts.

The *love feast* survives in the Eucharist, the central part of the mass when the priest raises up and consecrates the bread and wine, which thus become living parts of the body of God.

THE SYMBOLS OF PALÁCIO FOZ'S *ABADIA*

In the former *Abadia* (Abbey) restaurant in the cellar of Palácio Foz stands a curious full-size sculpture of a medieval architect. Wearing a Phrygian cap and supporting a column displaying two elephant heads with intertwined trunks, he represents the Grand Architect of the Temple of Virtue and Wisdom. The elephants represent the temple (one designates the wisdom of the spirit and the other the virtue of the soul). A Hindu icon of the god *Ganesh*, son of *Shiva*, the elephant is the patron of the *Gupta Vidya* or secret Wisdom.

Since he holds the secrets of the *Royal Art* (*Geometry* and *Mathematics*), the Master Architect is the keeper of wisdom and virtue. He is believed to be the perfect illustration of the *Royal Follower* or *Perfect Man*, keeper of the *Sacerdotal Art*, and builder of churches, cathedrals, palaces and castles throughout Europe.

Beneath the sculpture, a well is believed to descend into the bowels of Lisbon. To the right, a beautiful coral fountain symbolically represents the *fons de Sé* (fountain of Wisdom), from which the *Acqua Vitae* flows. This water purifies the body and inspires the soul of he who becomes the perfect Follower, as personified by the Grand Architect.

BAIRRO ALTO-SANTA CATARINA - CHIADO

THE FIVE-POINTED STAR OF GRANDELLA DEPARTMENT STORES ❶

Rua do Carmo
• Metro: Baixa-Chiado

Grandella, a former Freemason entrepreneur

Carved on the columns between the Grandella department store doors, the Grandella motto, "Always on the right path and moving forward", surrounds a five-pointed star. It is simply the Masonic star that Grandella adopted as his personal emblem. He had, in fact, been initiated to Freemasonry under the symbolic name of *Pilatos* and was affiliated to the *José Estevão* Lodge in Lisbon in 1910.

The *Amazéns Grandella* (Grandella department stores) have born the name of their owner, Francisco de Almeida Grandella (1852-1934) since 1891. A very wealthy businessman, Grandella arrived in Lisbon as a young man and grew rich thanks to his determination, honest work and sharp business sense.

After acquiring his first building in 1890, Grandella bought the building on rua do Carmo, located just behind his establishment, in 1903, and had it demolished in order to create a new structure and enlarge his store.

The majestic edifice was constructed by entrepreneur João Pedro dos Santos, after a design by French architect Georges Demay (who had designed the famous *Printemps* department stores in Paris). Engineer Ângelo de Sárrea Prado completed the project. In April 1907, the building, described by its owner as "… a gigantic, audacious, refined accomplishment whose richness, elegance, good taste, reflection of light, crystal, gilded capitals, marble columns make you think of fairytales, of the Thousand and One Nights!" was finally inaugurated. Lisbon now possessed the "most beautiful and largest department stores in the entire Iberian Peninsula."

The *Grandella Department Stores*, with their *Art Nouveau* style mixed with Portuguese decoration, thus opened to the public in 1907. After the great fire that destroyed the buildings in August 1980, the façade was restored. It was topped with a magnificent clock in which two blacksmiths sound the hours near the mythic figures of *Truth* and *Commerce* that had survived.

THE SYMBOLISM OF THE PENTAGRAM, THE FIVE-POINTED STAR

The *pentagram* is a five-pointed star composed of five straight lines. In Portuguese, *pentagrama* means a word with five letters. In music, it is also the five parallel lines that compose sheet music.

Originally, it was the symbol of the Roman goddess *Venus* and, consequently, was associated with this planet as its orbit, as seen from Earth, apparently draws a five-pointed star every eight years, as illustrated by the astronomer Ptolemy.

In nature, the *pentagram* is the sign of the fifth element, Ether, which occupies the superior branch, while the other four elements (Air, Fire, Water, Earth) occupy the inferior branches.

The pentagram (or *pentalpha*) is also the symbol for Infinity. In the pentagon at the centre of the pentagram, another smaller pentagram can be drawn, and so on.

It also possesses a numerical symbolism, always based on the number 5, which represents the marriage between the masculine (3) and the feminine (2), and thus symbolises the union of opposites that is necessary for spiritual realisation.

That is why, in the mathematics of the Pythagorean school of thought, the *pentagram* (the emblem of this Greek institution) is linked to the *golden ratio* (1.618). Composed of a regular pentagon and five isosceles triangles, the ratio between the side of the triangle and its base (the side of the pentagon) is equal to the *golden number*.

The Jewish Kabbalah, through its most learned rabbis, considers the *pentagram* to be the symbol of the will of God and of divine protection.

In Christianity, it is the star of Christmas and of Christ's birth, which predicts the Resurrection of both the spirit in the body (birth) and the body in the spirit (resurrection).

In Freemasonry, it is the Blazing Star of initiation. Placed in the eastern part of the Lodge, it also symbolises the resurrection, when the follower leaves the profane world to become a new initiate.

When the *pentagram* is shown upside-down, it generally becomes a symbol of Evil, the opposite of what it symbolises when upright (Good). It means that the Spirit has been plunged into the blindness of Matter and the physical suffering of the human soul.

THE SYMBOLS OF THE TOMB OF KING DOM FERNANDO I

②

Museum of Archaeology
Largo do Carmo
• Open Monday to Saturday, 10am to 5pm

> *A king
> in an alchemical
> tomb*

Damaged in the earthquake of 1755, which caused the building to collapse, the Gothic tomb of King Dom Fernando I (1345-1383) is now on exhibit at the city's Museum of Archaeology. In addition to the coats of arms of Portugal and of the Manuel family (his mother was Dona Constança Manuel), the tomb is covered in hermetic symbols.

Dom Fernando I, who died on 23 October 1383 in Lisbon, ordered that he be dressed in a Franciscan habit and buried next to his mother at the São Francisco convent at Santarém. His remains were left here, however, in the former Carmel convent founded in 1389 by the Saint Constable Dom Nuno Álvares Pereira, which was later converted into a museum.

The king's affinities and closeness to the *Beguins** explains the presence of elements connected to them on this funerary monument that was nevertheless kept at the Carmelite site. On one side of the tomb, the scene of Saint Francis of Assisi's inspiration on Mount Alvernia is depicted. The saint is shown receiving the stigmata of the Lord, and next to him, there is a monastery and a staircase with a praying monk, a symbol of adoration, faith and obedience to the Franciscan order.

On the other side of the tomb, a curious seated figure attentively looks at a vase before him. A book lies at his feet and, behind him on either side, two shelves are lined with more vases. A symbol of an alchemical laboratory (*labor oratorium*), this illustration is related to the images below, two effigies of a monk and a lady (perhaps Dom Fernando's mother) who, in this context, symbolise the hermetic couple and the union of opposites that was indispensable to the realisation of the grand work of alchemy.

At the base of the tomb, two griffons with necks interlaced represent the alchemical *rebis*, another reminder of the necessary union of opposites for the realisation of the philosopher's stone, which itself is an allegory of the spiritual awakening that accompanies the fabrication of philosophical gold.

Contrary to King Dom Afonso V, nothing suggests that Dom Fernando I was an alchemist, even if he was undoubtedly close to several followers of this tradition.

Beguins: Franciscans (sometimes Dominicans) called the "spiritual ones" who professed the purity of the origins of Christianity, combined with the hermetic concepts originating in alchemy, which they considered to be the representation of the "path of perfection".

ROYAL DOOR OF OUR LADY OF THE VICTORY ❸ OF MOUNT CARMEL CONVENT

Largo do Carmo

A completely forgotten door and staircase

O n leaving the famous Santa Justa lift to reach Largo do Carmo, hardly anyone notices the curious, boarded-up door to the right, in front of which is a beautiful staircase leading nowhere. It nevertheless holds significant historic meaning.

The Our Lady of the Victory of Mount Carmel convent was once sited opposite the hill where São Jorge castle stands, on the slopes of which stood the royal palace and Sé Cathedral. Between the two hills lay what is now the Rossio district, known as the *Valverde* (Green Valley) in the 14th and 15th centuries. Having abandoned military life for his religious vocation, Saint Constable Dom Nuno Álvares Pereira had this convent built in 1389. He was absolutely determined that the main building of Carmel convent should be built at this precise spot, in Lisbon, despite the technical difficulties of reinforcing the steep slopes and constructing the foundations of the church choir. When the foundations gave way twice, Dom Nuno vowed to rebuild them in bronze if they gave way yet again. On the third attempt, the most reputable architects of Lisbon were hired: Afonso, Gonçalo and Rodrigo Eanes. Several master masons were also hired (Lourenço Gonçalves, Estevão Vasques, Lourenço Afonso, and João Lourenço), as were workers to prepare and apply the lime, a specialised task that was entrusted to the Jews Judas Acarron and Benjamin Zagas. As each obstacle was overcome, another appeared, but the building was finally finished, becoming the most remarkable Gothic edifice of its time.

The royal palace and convent stood face to face and the route from one to the other passed through this *porta real* (royal door), now forgotten. Its *fleur-de-lis* decoration (see p. 24) is the royal symbol, officially adopted by Dom João I, the first member of the Avis dynasty, whose protector was the Saint Constable.

Note the inscriptions on the stones near the ground in front of the door. These images of fish, animals and birds survived the terrible earthquake of 1755, as did the staircase that led to Campo de Valverde and the royal palace.

NO VI CENTENARIO
DO NASCIMENTO
DO
SANTO CONDESTÁVEL

THE SAINT CONSTABLE'S MAGIC SWORD ❹

Carmelite convent cloister
Largo do Carmo
• Metro: Baixa-Chiado
• Open Monday to Saturday, 10am to 6pm

A sword inspired by King Arthur's Excalibur

A curious sword is exhibited in the ruined cloister of the Convento do Carmo (Carmelite convent). Although an identical sword can be found above the side door of the Nossa Senhora dos Remédios chapel in Sertã, it is said that the original is the one displayed at Lisbon's Military Museum, near Santa Apolónia.

Measuring three inches at its widest point, the sword is straight and sharp; its hilt is brass and is encircled by a brass spiral design. Engraved on one side of the blade is the inscription *Excelsus super omnes gentes Dominicus* (God the Highest above men). Engraved on the other side are the name *Maria*, the words *Dom Nuno Álvaro* within a circle, and a countermark depicting a cross interlaced with flowers. The piercings and engravings on the blade, beyond their decorative aspect, make the sword lighter and thus easier to manipulate. These engravings are reminiscent of runes (the letters of early Icelandic *Edda* literature). In practice, the enemy's blade could get caught in the grooves, meaning he could easily find himself disarmed.

This sword belonged to Saint Constable Dom Nuno Álvares Pereira (1360-1431). Since his youth, he had been strongly influenced by the myths of the Knights of the Round Table and their quest for the Holy Grail, or the Holy Chalice, a symbol of Inspiration by the grace of the Holy Spirit.

As an adult, he chose a military career and distinguished himself as a valiant defender of the kingdom. Searching for a magic sword like *Excalibur*, the sword of the mythic King Arthur, Pereira took his old sword to Fernão Vaz, the armourer of Santarém. Upon returning the refurbished sword, the armourer told him, in a prophetic tone, that he could pay him for the work when he became the Count of Ourém. Once he had, indeed, become count, Dom Nuno generously reimbursed this armourer who, in addition to being a blacksmith, was also an alchemist and prophet.

Thanks to his blessed *Excalibur*, pointed towards the heavens in order to invoke its power, Dom Nuno Álvares Pereira secured Portugal's independence, which was threatened by Castile. He then laid down his sword to symbolise the sign of the cross and joined the Order of Carmelites until the end of his days, living the exemplary life of a monk-knight.

The Constable's mark – a cross and a star – can be seen on one side of the blade.

THE CARMELITES: AN ORDER INFLUENCED BY HERMETISM

The *Carmelite Order*, originally called the *Order of the Brothers of the good adventurous Virgin Mary of Mount Carmel*, was formed in 1206-1214 by a group of Latin laymen, probably former Crusaders, who were led by a man only known by the letter B (he was later identified as Brocardo). They lived in the region of Mount Carmel, a range of hills near Haifa, formerly known as Porfiria, in what is now Israel.

The word *carmel* means "garden". Many Christians lived on this hill as hermits according to the biblical tradition of the prophet Elijah who in the past had retreated into a cave to live in prayer and silence. Later, these penitent Christians received a rule of life from Saint Albert, Latin Patriarch of Jerusalem, who regrouped them into a typically hermetic order centred on Christ. The Carmelite rule was approved by Pope Honorius III in 1226, but the monks had to return to Western Europe, where they began spreading the *Hyperdulia*, the worship and veneration of Our Lady, thus becoming Europe's first Marian religious order.

At the beginning of the 14th century, the Carmelites arrived in Portugal and settled at Moura, in the Alentejo region. Saint Constable Nuno Álvares Pereira quickly befriended them due to his great devotion for the Virgin Mary. He even had the Carmelite Convent of Lisbon built to house the brotherhood. He himself entered the order at the end of his life as a penitent brother of the Carmelites of the Ancient Observance, its oldest branch.

Later, in 1593, the Discalced Carmelite Order was founded, the result of reforms carried out by Saint Theresa of Avila and Saint John of the Cross. The Carmelites also had a certain connection to the hermetic tradition, as certain historic events indicate. They disapproved of Pope Clement V (the moral assassin of the Order of the Templars) and supported the election of João XII, author of the *Bula Sabatina*. They also benefited from the protection of the Hospitaller Order of Saint John of Acre, the future Order of Malta. They were accused of confusing the Virgin Mary with Mary of Egypt, known for an alchemical process that bears her name – that of distilling water using fire, or the famous "bain-marie". Two enormous azulejo panels, once in the now-closed Piedade de Cascais convent, are now on display in the Castro Guimarães villa gardens. One of them incontestably proves the Carmelite Order's hermetic connection. It depicts the *Triumphal Procession* of the Virgin Mary in Glory seated on the Chariot, in front of which stand the archangels Michael and Gabriel (associated with the Sun and the Moon) and behind which is the procession of the "Sons of Mary", that is to say the followers of alchemy, the science of the Holy Spirit – Saint Antoine, Saint Isabelle of Portugal, Saint Isabelle of Hungary, Saint Albert the Great, Raimundo Lúlio and Arnaldo de Vilanova, among others. The angels flying above, each of which show a distinctive sign of Carmelite hermetism, such as the coat of arms in the lower section, add a final touch to the work.

THE STRANGE STORY OF THE BRAÇO DE PRATA (SILVER ARM)

In Moscavide, right next to the Quinta do Cabeço, stands the *Quita do Candeeiro* (Chandelier), which was the convent the Discalced Carmelites came to after their flight from Estrela convent, which had been annexed to Lisbon's basilica, in 1834. In their flight, the nuns took a curious 17th-century relic with them – the right arm of Saint Theresa of Avila kept in a silver reliquary. The cult of the relic was so strong that its memory survived in a local place name. *Braço de Prata* station used to be the stop for Ribatejo pilgrims on their way to Olivais to worship the saint. Around 1930, the Carmelites of Candeeiro donated the holy reliquary to the family of Spanish general Franco who took it to Avila. Since then, its worship has died out, but its memory survives in the name *Braço de Prata*.

THE FÁBRICA DE CERVEJA DA TRINDADE'S MASONIC FAÇADE

Largo Rafael Bordalo Pinheiro, 28-34
Metro: Baixa-Chiado

On Largo da Trindade, a stunning façade covered from top to bottom by polychrome azulejo panels depicts figures inspired by Freemason mythology. This building, restored after the earthquake of 1755, is the former convent of the *Santíssima Trindade* (Most Holy Trinity), an order founded at the end of the 12th century. Thanks to the protection of Queen Santa Isabel, the order took up residence here in 1325, in what was the largest construction of Lisbon at the time. When the Trinitarian brothers were dispersed in 1833 and the convent closed in 1834, the building was put up for sale.

Moreira, a proud Freemason

Moreira Garcia, a rich and proud Freemason, bought the building and had extensive work done. The most radical of his initiatives was to have the façade covered in azulejos by painter Luís Ferreira in 1863. The artist based his work on Masonic themes, as Moreira Garcia had requested. The same was done for the other panels created for the interior of his brasserie (see pp. 130-131).

The façade is a eulogy to Earth, Water, Commerce, Industry, Science and Agriculture. The introduction of lion heads is stunning. They are the heraldic symbol of both Moreira Garcia and the Order of the Trinity.

On the triangular moulding at the top, note the Radiant Star (see p. 117) in the centre and, inside, the Delta with the Eye of the Grand Architect of the Universe (see following double page).

In 1834, the *Fábrica de Cerveja da Trindade* (Brewery of the Trinity) was installed in the monks' former refectory and in a section of the cloister. In 1836, on rua Nova da Trindade, the *Cervejaria Trindade* (Trinity brasserie) was created and became the official brewery of the royal family. It quickly became one of the most sought-after locations in Lisbon and is the country's oldest brewery. In 1934, the brewery and restaurant were bought by the Central de Cerveja Corporation and the site was taken over by the group in 1935.

THE EYE OF THE TRIANGLE

The eye of the triangle tradition, which can be seen in most Christian temples, has its origin in the first apostolic preachers of Christianity. It was inherited from pharaonic Egypt as preserved in Persian writings that Christians collected in Alexandria, in Egypt. The central, radiant Sun god (*Ra*) was replaced by the Eye of Divine Providence enveloped in a luminous aura of glory covering the Triangle (Luminous Delta).

Whereas for the ancient Egyptians the equilateral triangle represented the *Osirian Triad* of Osiris – Horus – Isis, for the Christians it became the Holy Trinity of the Father – Son – Holy Spirit. Viewed as one indivisible Being incarnated by the Eye or Sun of Egypt, it is often replaced by the name of God, *Jehovah*, and generally broken down into four Hebraic letters, *Iod-He-Vau-Heth*.

It is through its equal sides and angles that the equilateral Triangle symbolises the Most Holy Trinity, or rather, three Hypostases emanating from the unique Logos expressed by the Sun of Egypt or "All-Seeing Eye", a way of saying that the Absolute rules over the entire Universe.

The presence of the Trinity and the Triangle is practically universal, as it is found in most traditional religions – in the Hindu *Trimurti* (Trinity) manifested by Brahma – Vishnu – Shiva, but especially in ancient Egypt where this symbol appeared over several eras of its history. Beside the *Osirian Triad*, there was the *Memphite Triad* of Ptah – Nefertem – Sekhmet (Father – Son – Mother) and the *Theban Triad* of Amon – Khonsu – Mut, the primordial gods of this civilisation's pantheon. In Persia, there was Ahura Mazda – Vohu Mano – Asha Vahista, that is the Master Sage, Good Thought and Best Rectitude. It was this trinity that served as the inspiration for the one conceived by the Christians.

In the 18th century, with the appearance of speculative Freemasonry, the Masons immediately adopted this symbol, calling it the Luminous Delta. Their symbol depicted a Sun, an Eye or simply a G in the centre, representing the Grand Architect of the Universe, the Divinity that created everything and everyone, the supreme Surveyor.

Sometimes Freemasons replace the Triangle by three dots (one at each point of the triangle) that signify the Past, Present and Future, while the full triangle represents Eternity or the Eternal God. The three angles thus represent the three phases of the perpetual evolution of existence: Birth – Life – Death, an evolution that God governs without being governed.

In short, the radiant Eye of the Triangle is the emblem of the Divinity that is Una (unique) in its essence and Trina (threefold) in its manifestation. For this reason it is considered to be the expression of the Perfect Spirit and of the True Initiate united in a Triune God.

TRINDADE BRASSERIE'S MASONIC AZULEJOS ❻

Rua Nova da Trindade, 20C
Open daily, 10am to 8pm
• Metro: Baixa-Chiado

> *Manuel Garcia Moreira, master mason, third degree*

The refectory and part of the cloister of the former Lisbon Trinitarian convent are now the *Cervejaria Trindade* (Trinity Brasserie), one of the most distinguished restaurants in the city. On entering, you cannot fail to notice a series of polychrome azulejo panels along the wall clearly depicting Masonic themes.

Their creator, painter Luís Ferreira, the artistic director of the Viúva de Lamego factory (see p. 231), was better known as "Ferreira das Tabuletas" (Shop Sign Ferreira) (1807-1870). He has left a rare example of his naive and popular style here. The saturated colours in strong chromatic contrasts are set in false recesses, like statue niches, thus imitating *trompe l'oeil* painting.

It was the Galician Manuel Garcia Moreira who commissioned these panels from the artist after having bought the building of the former Trinity convent from Joaquim Peres in 1836. A converted Freemason, Garcia Moreira had azulejo panels made for his garden, the building's lateral façade, and the interior of the convent's former rectory. The *lion's head* symbol, repeated in profusion throughout the work, designates the third degree in the Masonic hierarchy, that of master mason.

The *lion's claws*, a symbol of the same rank that designates the resurrection of Hiram Abiff, the Phoenician architect of King Solomon's Temple, also occurs frequently.

In the above-mentioned false niches, there are other Masonic symbols, such as the allegorical representations of the luminous delta with the eye of the Supreme Architect inscribed in a radiant sun. On another panel, the goddess *Concordia*, shown holding a rod and offering an olive branch to a dove, is the symbol of Concord (Universal Brotherhood). The column of *force* (*Bohaz*), featured on Solomon's Temple, was adopted into Masonic symbolism. It also appears, supported by a seated woman (passive); at her feet is a lion's head rising out of the clouds, symbolising Garcia Moreira himself.

AQVI ESTA EM PÉ O CORPO Đ DOM
FRANCISCO TREGIAN FIDALGO IN
GRES MVI ILLVSTRE·O QVAL ĐPOIS
DE COFISCADOS SEVS ESTADOS·E
GRANDES TRABALHOS PADECÍ
DOS EM·2̃·8·ANNOS ĐPRISAM POHA
DE FÉ Đ̃A DA FE CATOLICA EM ĨNG̃A
NA PERSEGVÇAM DA RAINHA ISA
BEL NO ANNO DE 1608 A 2 5 DE
MOPREO NESTA CIDADE DE LISBOA
COM GRANDE FAMA Đ SANTIDA
DE·AVENDO 17 ANNOS Q ESTAVA
SEPVLTAIĐ NESTA IGREIA DE
S·ROQVE DA COMP̃A DE IHŠ NO
DE 1625·AOS·25·DE ABRIL SE A
CHOV SEV CORPO INTEIRO E
ĨNCORRVPTO E FOI COLLOCAIĐ
NESTE LVGAR PELLOS INGRE. SE S
CATOLICOS RESIDĒT ES NESTA
CIDADE·AOS 25 Đ ABRIL DE·1626

TOMBS OF THE SEBASTIANISTS

São Roque church
Largo Trindade Coelho
• Opening times: Monday to Saturday, 10am to 6pm
• Metro: Baixa-Chiado

> *Mystics who believed in the return of King Sebastian*

Built at the end of the 16th century based on plans drawn up by architect Felipe Terzi for the site of the hermitage of the same name, the monumental *São Roque* (Saint Roch) church was granted to the Jesuits by Dom João III. This church of impressive artistic splendour was strongly marked in the past by the presence of the inspired Sebastianists, a blend of prophets, visionaries and saints, as the miraculous relics venerated in the side altar demonstrate.

Some inspired Jesuits also propagated millenarian myths, including Father António Vieira who preached in this very place his famous *Sermão das 40 horas* (40-hour sermon), revealing part of his theories regarding the Fifth Empire (see p. 70).

In the 16th and 17th centuries, numerous "prophet cobblers" appeared. Nicknamed the "*bandarra*", they were endowed with the gift of prophecy for the past, present and future. One of them, Simão Gomes, is buried in the church in front of the altar to the Virgin. At the time of Dom Sebastião, when he was a member of the Council of State, he poured out inspired prophecies that, when put into practice, were of great political use. He died in a state of grace in October 1576.

The grave of another Sebastianist, Dom Francisco Tregian, can be found half-way along the left side of the building. This Englishman, who was reputed for his great saintliness, died on 25 December 1608. He had adopted Lisbon as his new home at a young age.

The spiritual vocation of these individuals is perfectly reflected in Saint Roch, who is described as a pilgrim whose knee is visible and who is accompanied by a dog. The pilgrim is the image of someone searching for knowledge by following the initiatory path of knowledge that he discovers step by step. The dog is the animal of the wise man, the follower's companion who protects him on the path of his choice. The uncovered left knee is the unequivocal sign of initiation, an initiation that is often identified with the circle of the compass that is used to trace the plans of the house of God. Revealing the kneecap attracts the attention of the one who knows to the one who reveals.

Is it perhaps for this undisclosed reason that Dom João V, rapidly proclaimed the "king of the Fifth Empire," ordered this church's treasure – the chapel of Saint John the Baptist, Christ's prophet – from Rome in 1742?

SEBASTIANISM AND MESSIANISM

Strictly speaking, *Messianism* is the prophetic belief of the universal coming or return of a holy liberator, a *Messiah* (*Mashiah* in Hebrew, *Christos* in Greek, *Avatara* in Hindu).

Sebastianism is a mystic movement that appears patriotic and grew during the second half of the 16th century following the death of King *Dom Sebastião* at the battle of Ksar el-Kebir in 1578 (see p. 105). As he had no heir, the Portuguese throne fell into the hands of King Felipe II, of the Spanish branch of the Habsburg family. *Sebastianism* is an Iberian form of *Messianism* adapted to this situation that was dramatic for the Portuguese. This tradition expresses their refusal of the established political situation and their hope for a way out, undoubtedly a miraculous one. According to common belief, the king was simply hidden (*encoberto*), waiting somewhere for the right time to return to Portugal, take back his throne and push out the occupying Spanish forces.

The most popular propagator of *Sebastianism* was the cobbler of the city of Trancoso, Gonçalo Anes, nicknamed *Bandarra* (1500-1556), who predicted the return of the *Desired King* (as Dom Sebastião was also called) in popular verse.

The main intellectual figure adhering to the movement was, nevertheless, Father António Vieira (1608-1697) (see p. 72), who developed the theme in depth.

Portuguese poet Fernando Pessoa (1888-1935), in his book of patriotic poems entitled *Mensagem*, also provided a reinterpretation and eulogy of the history of Portugal enlightened by Sebastianism, thus aiming to unite the country's historic past to its spiritual future.

Sebastianism, the belief of the return of the lost Dom Sebastião, was thus linked to the already existing *Messianism* by adding the hagiography of Saint Sebastian the martyr (see p. 213).

GONÇALO ANE
BANDARRA
SEC. XVI
POETA, PROFETA E SAPATEIRO
DE TRANCOSO
29-05-2001

MESSIANISM AND THE FIFTH EMPIRE

Some empower the Messiah in a much wider way, believing he is destined for all humanity and to inaugurate a new evolutionary cycle on a planetary scale. He will manifest himself by attitudes resulting from the feeling of being "elected" or "called" to accomplish a "holy" task. During the reign of Dom João V, this led to the distinction between the new Patriarchal church of Lisbon, which represented the future, and the old Episcopal church of Rome, representing the past. Here, we find the theme of the *translatio imperii* with the future *Fifth Empire* (see p. 70).

FADO: PORTUGUESE IDENTITY LINKED TO SEBASTIANISM?

In his philosophical theories, Fernando Pessoa united the elements of theosophy and the idea of Destiny, or *fado* (*fatum* in Latin), to make Messianic Sebastianism a unique characteristic of Portuguese cultural identity.

CAGLIOSTRO AT PALÁCIO SOBRAL ❽

Largo do Calhariz, beginning of Calçada do Combro

> **The place where Mozart's "Magic Flute" was played for Cagliostro**

The fact that Alessandro Cagliostro, count of Fénix (see opposite), spent time in Lisbon is largely unknown. However, Cagliostro played a determining role in Portuguese Freemasonry. After a journey from Rome to Santiago de Compostela, Cagliostro arrived in Lisbon on 25 April 1787, accompanied by his wife, Serafina Feliciani. They lodged at the Café Central in rua de Remolares on the cais do Sodré. After receiving an invitation from the Sobrais brothers, the couple took up residence at the Palácio Sobral, which Joaquim Inácio da Cruz Sobral had acquired after making his fortune in Salvador da Bahia, Brazil, thanks to his brother José Francisco da Cruz, who had introduced him to business affairs. The Sobral family also had close connections with the marquis of Pombal. The parties and literary salons at Palácio Sobral were memorable. It was in this enlightened milieu that Cagliostro made his entrance. A few months later, in 1788, the illustrious count of Saint-Germain, a Rosicrucian Grand Master, and his wife Lorenza Feliciani also arrived in Lisbon with a delegation from the embassy of Venice. It was in this palace that Cagliostro and Serafina initiated Joaquim Inácio da Cruz Sobral and his sister, Ana Joaquina da Cunha Sobral, into the mysteries of Egyptian Freemasonry. On 2 August 1887, the palace was finally sold by its last private owner, the marquis of Sousa Holstein, to the *Caixa Geral de Depósitos* (a state-owned banking corporation). No sooner had the transaction taken place than a fire broke out, almost destroying the entire premises, which is why the bank did not move in until 15 February 1947, after a complete renovation.

EGYPTIAN MYSTERIES REVEALED IN *THE MAGIC FLUTE*

It was in the luxurious rooms of Palácio Sobral that Mozart's *Magic Flute* was played for the first time in Portugal, around 1793. Mozart had dedicated the work to his master *Sarastro*, referring to *Cagliostro* who had formerly spent some time there. The name *Sarastro* means "fifth star" (Venus) and it figures in the opera's libretto with the same spelling, just like the name Hierophant, taken from the Egyptian mysteries that this work transposes into music in brilliant fashion. Wolfgang Amadeus Mozart received his initiatory knowledge from Cagliostro in person, after being initiated into the "Charity" Masonic Lodge of Vienna, Austria, on 14 December 1784. The premiere of *The Magic Flute* took place on 30 September 1791, also in Vienna.

CAGLIOSTRO, AN OCCULTIST WHO INSPIRED MOZART, GOETHE AND ALEXANDRE DUMAS

A master of the occult arts and sciences, alchemist and therapist, Alessandro Cagliostro was born in Palermo in 1743 and died in Rome in 1795. He is generally associated with Giuseppe Balsamo, an individual about whom little is known, besides the fact that he was a traveller and alchemist who had spent his childhood at the monastery of Caltagirone, in Sicily. Alessandro Cagliostro is believed to have been raised by the Tavernays, a noble French family. His biological father, Cardinal Emmanuel of Rohan, Master of the Order of Malta, supposedly conceived him during a moment of weakness with the marquise of Tavernay, but he abandoned the child. During his childhood, Cagliostro was apparently taken to Egypt and educated in a monastery of the Coptic Church; he was thus in contact with the monastery's spiritual Masters. From there, he is believed to have travelled to India and Tibet. On his way back to Europe, he visited the Middle East: Egypt, Arabia, Persia, Rhodes and Malta. In Messina or Rhodes, he supposedly met the count of Saint-Germain, who initiated him in the mysteries of the hermetic tradition. In Malta, he was regularly seen at the court of Manuel Pinto, a native of Portugal and the new Grand Master of the Military Order of the Knights of Saint John of Malta. Thanks to Maltese influence, he made his first appearance in Rome as a count and frequented the noblest Italian families. There, he met Serafina Feliciani, who later became his wife. In 1772, Cagliostro and his wife settled in France. They were known to be benefactors for the poor, therapists for the needy and prodigious Masters of the Holy Science. In Lyon, Cagliostro founded the first Lodge of his so-called Egyptian Freemasonry (androgynous or Coptic), and popularised it throughout France, England, Germany, Holland, Poland and Russia, with phenomenal success, thanks to his great charisma and vast knowledge of occult sciences. These attributes gained him entrance to all the European courts and, in particular, that of French King Louis XVI. Cagliostro warned the king of the Revolution that was about to break out and of the danger threatening the royal family. In 1785, he was involved in Queen Marie-Antoinette's famous "diamond necklace affair". Accused of stealing the necklace, he was imprisoned in the Bastille, where he wrote his memoirs. The Parisian police eventually proved Cagliostro's innocence and he was freed. In Rome, The Inquisition imprisoned him for heresy in 1789. Condemned to death in 1791, his sentence was commuted to life imprisonment at the castle of San Leo. It is said that he died there from disease and poor medical treatment in 1795. Yet it is also claimed that he was secretly removed from the prison and sent to North America, along with his wife. As regards her fate, it is said that she was also condemned to reclusion for life in a religious convent, but these claims are found only in Jesuit documents. Along with the count of Saint-Germain, Alessandro Cagliostro was one of the most extraordinary figures of the 18th century, so extraordinary, in fact, that Mozart dedicated his work *The Magic Flute* (1768) to him, Goethe used his life as inspiration for his drama *Der Grosskophta* (1792), and Alexandre Dumas made him the hero of his novel *Memoirs of a Physician* (1846).

PALÁCIO DO MANTEIGUEIRO ⑨

Rua da Horta Seca, 15
• Metro: Chiado
• Visit on request at the palace

> *A miser's hidden splendours*

The *Palácio do Manteigueiro* (Butter Merchant's Palace), or *Palácio Condeixa*, where the Ministry of Energy is now located, is connected to *rua das Chagas* (Wounds street) by a gate giving access to a passage leading to the garden behind the building.

Originally, the palace only had one floor with a sloping roof, and two other ground-floor wings on the side facing *rua da Emenda*, due to the slope. The three upper floors were added later. On the exterior, note the stonework of the balcony windows of the second floor; the central window bears the coat of arms of the viscount of Condeixa. Also note the main gate, the courtyard, the square paved with black and white marble stones, as well as the main staircase, quite remarkable despite having been stripped of its former ornamentation, and the chapel on the second floor displaying magnificent sculpted wood and a beautiful dome.

The interior was impressively elegant. The doors of Brazilian wood were covered in damask and the ceilings painted by Pedro Alexandrino (1730-1810). The crystal mirrors were framed in pure gold "obtained by melting gold objects".

Manuel Caetano de Sousa seems to have been behind the project for this palace, which dates back to 1787 and was built by Domingos Mendes Dias, a native of the Trás-os-Montes region.

DOMINGOS MENDES DIAS, A TRUE MISER

Domingos Mendes Dias was a curious man. After running away from his parents' home to come to Lisbon, he worked as a water carrier and apprentice salesman. Involved in dubious affairs relating to the expulsion of Jesuits from the kingdom, he ended up quite rich. After the earthquake of 1755, he emigrated to Brazil where he increased his wealth and even obtained a noble title. The palace's name came from his business of selling butter in bulk. An extremely rich man, Domingos Mendes Dias was a true miser. He lived alone with an old female servant. It is said that he had his dinner served in the drawer of his writing desk so that he could close it if an unexpected visitor arrived. His greatest pleasure was "making up cartons of one hundred gold coins". Refusing to spend money on medicine, he died of gangrene in his own bed, having been stabbed during an attempted robbery. At his death in 1836, the palace became the headquarters of the *Assembleia Lisbonense* of the partisans of the *Carta constitucional* (Constitutional Charter).

SAINT CATHERINE'S CHURCH

Calçada do Combro, 82
Santa Catarina parish
• Open Monday to Saturday, 10am to 12pm and 3pm to 5pm

> **Fathers**
> **of the Desert**
> **in Santa Catarina**

A destination of constant pilgrimage, Santa Catarina church possesses one of Lisbon's most beautiful artistic, cultural, religious and historical heritages.

This imposing church of the former convent of the Saint Paul the Hermit monks of Serra de Ossa, in the Alentejo region, dominates the Calçada do Combro district, near the former Santa Catarina do Monte Sinai Church (founded by Queen Catherine of Austria on 27 May 1557 and ravaged by fire in 1835). Built in 1647, this church later inherited the ruins of the old Santa Catarina church, as well as those of the Santo Espirito do Recolhimento dos Cardais chapel, destroyed in the earthquake of 1755.

Upon entering this sumptuous building, visitors are immediately overwhelmed by its imposing sobriety that corresponds to the vocation of the recluse life of the monks of Saint Paul the Hermit (3rd century AD), who came from Alentejo. Also known as the Hermits of Serra de Ossa, these monks rebuilt this church under the name of the Holy Sacrament and left to posterity the apocryphal cult (they are not in the four synoptic gospels) of Saint Joachim and Saint Anne, believed to be the parents of the Virgin, by clearly showing them on the Baroque-style side altar made of gilded wood.

On the side walls hang large paintings in carved and gilded frames, depicting cenobite* saints venerated by the Hermits of Saint Paul – men and women considered to be visionaries, prophets, and in some cases enlightened ones. The titles of these paintings attributed to Bento Coelho da Silveira and André Gonçalves, 17th- and 18th-century artists, thus mention Saint Malachy, Saint Mary the Egyptian, Saint Anthony and Saint Thais, to name but a few.

The term "Fathers of the Desert" corresponds to the reclusion that was characteristic of early Christianity, as well as to the cenobitic "desert" of retreating from the profane world. The Saint Paul of the Desert hermits made this choice and thus participated in the *sacerdotal art* (see p. 62).

*cenobite: member of a monastic community

ADAMASTOR
(O VELHO DO RESTELO)

THE SCULPTURE OF ADAMASTOR

Belvedere of Alto de Santa Catarina

> *A symbol*
> *of the superstitions*
> *of certain*
> *Sebastianists*

At Alto de Santa Catarina stands a strange sculpture by Júlio Vaz Júnior dating from 1927, the meaning of which is often forgotten today.

The statue depicts *Adamastor*, a monstrous mythical figure imagined by Luís de Camões in his work *Os Lusíadas*. Adamastor was a terrifying sea god who lived near Cape Boujdour, on the African coast, and who swallowed up the ships that came near him. He was thus a kind of ogre used by the Portuguese naval fleet in the 15th century to keep the superstitious ships of other countries from following them on the maritime routes they used and that only they knew. In *Mensagem*, Fernando Pessoa called him *Mostrengo* (Great Monster).

SANTA CATARINA: A BELVEDERE FOR THE LOST

"Watch the ships from the top of Santa Catarina" is a popular 19th-century Portuguese expression dating from 1807. During the French invasions, the demoralised people stood on the heights of Santa Catarina to watch the ships carrying the royal family leave the Tagus estuary, on their way to the Brazilian royal court.

The country thus abandoned and left to despair, only one solution remained: turn towards the Bandarra prophecies that the highly respected Father António Vieira had popularised. It was at this time that Alto de Santa Catarina, near Calçada do Combro, became a curious hideout for lost Sebastianists (see p. 134) who gathered, in a sort of urban "new age" movement, without judgment or organisation, equipped with telescopes pointed at the estuary, hoping to see the arrival of the ship of the long-awaited King Dom Sebastião. They did not know if he would arrive from Africa, Brazil, or some unknown island hidden in the ocean ... and this tradition has survived, not largely followed, but still alive.

This is the origin of *red Sebastianism*, better known as royal millenarianism, a political trend based on all sorts of prophecies and that sees symbols and signs in everything that is social and immediate, with much incoherence and ridicule.

There is also *white Sebastianism*, which is completely different, being enlightened and holding metaphysical meaning. Although more coherent, it is the lesser-known aspect of Portuguese millenarianism (see p. 134).

THE BOTANICAL GARDEN'S BUTTERFLY HOUSE

Rua da Escola Politécnica, 58
• Metro: Rato
• Open Monday to Friday, 9am to 8pm; Saturday, Sunday and public holidays, 10am to 8pm

Curiosities of the Botanical Garden

The *Jardim Botânico de Lisboa* (Lisbon's Botanical Garden) possesses unequalled historic, cultural and scientific significance. Covering four hectares, it contains plants from Portugal, Europe, the other continents and the Atlantic islands. The historic collections date back to the 18th century and are the result of expeditions and voyages to Africa, Brazil, Asia and Timor. The seeds of rare and threatened species are preserved here in the *Banco das Sementes* (Seed Bank).

The magnificent and luxurious flora of this marvellous site conceals a butterfly house at its centre, the only one in Europe open to the public. This greenhouse is officially called the *Lagartagis* to remind visitors that the

butterflies were once caterpillars (*lagartas*). The idea is to show the public the butterfly's life cycle, from reproduction, to birth as a caterpillar, to the formation of the chrysalis that will one day reveal a new butterfly. The greenhouse is equipped with air-conditioning to maintain the spring-like temperature that favours the insects' procreation and reproduction.

The garden also abounds with aromatic plants, as their scent is very important for the butterflies.

Besides the garden, the complex is home to the Science Museum and the Natural History Museum whose team, originally directed by professor Galopim de Carvalho, has succeeded in bringing Europe's most important exhibitions on dinosaurs to the museum.

LAPA - ESTRELA - CAMPO DE OURIQUE

THE HIGH RELIEF OF MARTYR SAINTS

Igreja de Santos o Velho
Rua das Janelas Verdes
• Bus: 60

> **Lisbon's "Saint James' Way"**

Near the entrance to *Santos o Velho* (Santos the Old) church, an ancient stonework depicts three people, each holding a staff. It shows the brother and sisters Veríssimo, Máxima and Júlia, the martyr saints to whom the church is dedicated. Inside, you can also find an altar devoted to them, with statues to worship them and beautiful azulejo panels illustrating their life story.

Originally from Lisbon, the three were martyred on 1 October 307, on the order of Roman emperor Diocletian, for having refused to make a sacrifice to the gods. After their death, heavy stones were tied to them and they were thrown into the sea, but their bodies drifted to a beach near Lisbon. Christian hermits piously gathered them up and buried them in a church erected in their honour, called *Santos* (Saints). It is said that, for a long time after, oval pebbles tainted with blood and engraved with a Saint James Cross appeared on Santos beach.

The church founded by Dom Afonso Henriques came into existence thanks to his daughter, Dona Sancha. Led to the spot by the hand of an angel, she discovered the relics that gave off a particularly pleasant scent (see below). It is interesting to note that this story strangely resembles the legend of Saint James, in which the apostle's tomb is also discovered thanks to angels and a shower of stars. In 1290, Dom Sancho II enlarged the church and had a convent built for the *Ordem de Santiago* (Order of Saint James), as well as for the women, children and widows of these monk knights. These women elected a *comendadeira* or *dona* (lady), whence the origin of the *Comendadeiras de Santos*, who were later sent to Coimbra before returning here. As the convent was too small, Dom João II had another one built for them in 1470, at Xabregas, naming it *Santos o Novo* (Santos the New). All the nuns were moved there on 5 September 1490. The relics of the martyr saints were transported in a golden coffer in procession and placed in a small chapel dedicated to *Nossa Senhora do Paraíso* (Our Lady of Paradise).

IN THE ODOUR OF SANCTITY

The pleasant scent that is sometimes emitted from the bodies of certain saints is at the origin of the expression "in the odour of sanctity".

SECRETS OF NUNO GONÇALVES' POLYPTYCH ❷

Museu Nacional de Arte Antiga
Rua das Janelas Verdes
• Open Tuesday 2pm to 6pm and Wednesday to Sunday 10am to 6pm
Closed Monday
• Bus: 60

A coded message?

On show at the *Museu Nacional de Arte Antiga* (National Museum of Ancient Art), Nuno Gonçalves' polyptych (comprising two large panels and four narrower ones) is a masterpiece of Portuguese painting from the end of the Middle Ages and beginning of the Renaissance. Its creator, Nuno Gonçalves, royal artist for Dom Afonso V from 1450 onwards, is believed to have died in 1492.

It is said that this polyptych, of a rather sober yet strongly realistic style, was painted at the *Paço Real* (Royal Palace) of Sintra. It was not discovered until 1882, when Rafael Bordalo Pinheiro and his sister realised that workers were using it as scaffolding during restoration work on the patriarchate of São Vicente de Fora. They saved it from destruction without delay and began to restore it. However, it was not until 1931, when the work was exhibited in Paris, that Nuno Gonçalves won the international recognition he deserved. In a superb yet enigmatic manner, the polyptych illustrates the entire Lusitanian epic of the Avis dynasty. The 60 figures portrayed in the work have given rise to endless debates regarding their identification and placement, as well as the correct order of the panels.

The first panel is that of the *Monks*, shown dressed in the attire of the Cistercian Order, and the second, that of the *Navigators*, which shows crown prince Henrique kneeling at the front. In the centre of the third panel, that of the *Pontiff*, is a saint that resembles the Coptic and Byzantine representations of Prester John (Melkitzedek), King of Salem (representing heaven on earth) and priest of God Most High (representing the celestial paradise), and not, as some biblical scholars have claimed, Saint Vincent, Saint Catherine, the crown prince Dom Ferdinand, or the cardinal of Lisbon, James of Portugal. As in the scriptures, the saint is shown with the Gospel of Saint John open at the Pentecostal mass (see following double page). The same saint is found on the *Monarch* panel (the fourth), holding the King of the World's sceptre; the ropes at his feet outline a map of Portugal. The fifth panel is that of the *Knights*, and the sixth that of the *Relic*, showing a bone from the skull of Saint Anthony of Lisbon and Padua. Sixty figures are portrayed in all: 6 in the first panel, 7 in the second, 34 in the third and fourth, 8 in the fifth and 5 in the sixth. According to ancient Kabbalistic numerology, the number 60 represents *Evolution*. By dividing it by the double 3, and ignoring the zero that represents the abstract or nothingness, one obtains the Holy Trinity on earth and in the heavens and towards which all living things strive.

Two other important numbers are 13 (illustrated in the number of figures portrayed in the first two and last two panels) and 17 (the number of characters in each of the central panels). The number 13 symbolises the *Immortality* of the human soul after death. It is also the number that is traditionally attributed to Saint Mary and the Holy Spirit, to whom Portugal (*Porto-Graal* – see page 20) is dedicated.

The number 17 symbolises the hope for Immortality that the Word of God (as revealed in the open copy of the Gospel of Saint John) transmits to the congregation or, in other words, all of humanity. The number 17 also has a special meaning for Portugal. It is its own esoteric arcanum and designates the country as the ultimate hope for a new global spiritual empire (see page 102).

In addition to a sword and a pair of scales, the iconic symbols of Melkitzedek, King of the World (see p. 152), include the episcopal cross and book, which represent the Temporal and Spiritual powers. The polyptych's saint bears exactly these symbols.

Arrangement of the figures in the polyptych:

17 =	3	3	11	11	4	2	= 17
13 =	3	4	6	6	4	3	= 13

	=			=	
13		17	17		13

MELKI-TZEDEK AND PRESTER JOHN: MYTH AND REALITY

According to Judaeo-Christian tradition, the name *Melkitzedek*, earlier known as *Melki-Tzedek*, refers to the role of "King of the World". In charge of the Earth's evolution, he is the closest to God, and his function joins with that of God.

In the Bible, the first reference to *Melki-Tzedek* appears in Genesis 14:18-20. "And Melchizedek king of Salem brought forth bread and wine: and he was the priest of the most high God. And he blessed him, and said, Blessed be Abram of the most high God ... And he gave him tithes of all." This thus established the Order mentioned in Psalms 110:4: "Thou art a priest for ever after the order of Melchizedek." In Hebrews 7:1-3, Saint Paul describes it as follows: "For this Melchizedek, king of Salem, priest of the most high God, who met Abraham ... and blessed him; To whom also Abraham gave a tenth part of all; first being by interpretation King of righteousness, and after that also King of Salem, which is, King of peace; Without father, without mother, without descent, having neither beginning of days, nor end of life; but made like unto the Son of God; abideth a priest continually."

This is why the Christian Church identified him with the Third Person of the Trinity, the Holy Spirit, and with the guardian of the apostolic tradition that began with Peter the Apostle, so much so, in fact, that the *Sacrifice of Melki-Tzedek* (bread and wine) is generally seen as a "foreshadowing" of the Eucharist. Theoretically, Christian priests identify with the *priesthood of Melki-Tzedek*, as Psalm 110 also applies to Christ.

By referring to this mysterious king, the books of Genesis and Hebrews led the Judaeo-Christian tradition to distinguish between two priesthoods: one "according to the Order of Aaron", and the other "according to the Order of *Melki-Tzedek*". The latter is superior to the former as it connects the present to the time of the coming of the Messiah and is related to the apostles, bishops and the Western Church. Aaron, on the other hand, connects the past to the present through the prophets, patriarchs and the Eastern Church.

Melki-Tzedek is thus both king and priest. His name means "king of Righteousness" and king of *Salem*, or "king of Peace", "Righteousness" and "Peace" being exactly the two fundamental attributes of the "King of the World". The word *Salem* designates the "City of Peace," the archetype according to which *Jerusalem* was built, and which became the secret residence of the "King of the World". In the trans-Himalayan tradition, this city is called *Agharta* or *Shambala* and corresponds to the Terrestrial Paradise or the Primordial *Eden* that the Lusitanian myth insistently identifies with the future Fifth Empire of the World (see p. 70) which will mark the coming of the Kingdom of Happiness, ruled by *Melki-Tzedek*, the Universal Emperor.

The equivalent of *Melki-Tzedek* in Ancient Egypt was *Ptah*; in India, he is called *Chakravarti*. The Rosicrucians knew him as *Rotan*, which is why the Freemasons recognised him under the name of *Incognito Superior*, or the *Universal Emperor*, in the 18th century.

In the 12th century, in France, under the reign of Saint Louis, Carpin and Rubruquis in their travel accounts replaced the name of *Melki-Tzedek* with that of *Preste João* (*Father* or *Prester John*), who supposedly lived in a mysterious country at the northern edge of Asia. *Preste* means "Father" and "Priest" while *John* is a reference both to John the Baptist and John the evangelist who wrote the *Apocalypse*, a clear reference to the King of the World priesthood. The three religions of the Book (Judaism, Christianity and Islam) equally declare that it is through him that the Kingdom of Universal Harmony will come to Earth.

Word of Prester John first arrived in Europe in 1145, when Hugo de Gebel, a bishop of the Christian colony in what is now Lebanon, told the pope of the existence of a Christian kingdom located "beyond Persia and Armenia" that was ruled by a king-priest called *Johannes Presbyter* (John the Priest, the Father, or the Ancient). He was supposedly the descendent of one of the Three Kings that went to see the Baby Jesus in Bethlehem.

The first known document from this mysterious individual is the famous *Letter of Prester John*, sent to Manuel I Comnenus, Byzantine emperor of Constantinople, as well as to Frederick I Barbarossa, emperor of Germany, and to Pope Alexander III. The document apparently came from Portugal. The oldest version of the original text can be found in the Alcobaça monastery library and dates from the end of the 14th century. Published for the first time in Italian, at Venice in 1478, the letter inspired other Italian works, such as the rhymed version *Tratacto del maximo Prete Janni* (Venice?, 1494) by Giuliano Dati. In roughly the same period, Marco Polo, who had just returned to Venice, mentioned the existence of a Priest John, whom he believed to be the sovereign of the Ethiopian Church. Throughout the 15th and 16th centuries, another series of letters from Prester John appeared, this time sent from India to Portuguese rulers (João II, Manuel I and even Sebastião I, who is also said to have welcomed an ambassador sent by Prester John in his palace in Lisbon). The Portuguese kings also sent ambassadors to

Prester John's court, as was notably the case for Pêro da Covilhã, sent by Dom Afonso V.

The myth of Prester John was widely spread by the Knights Templar and constituted a strong impetus for Portugal's maritime discoveries. Although the apparent purpose of this exploration was to encourage the Christian conquest of new lands and obtain great riches, in fact, it was to establish a connection between Portugal and the Primordial Centre of the World, otherwise known as *Salem* or *Shamballah*.

SYMBOLISM OF THE TWO-HEADED MANUELINE FOUNTAIN

Museu Nacional de Arte Antiga
• Opening times: Tuesday 2pm-6pm, Thursday to Sunday 10am-6pm
Closed Monday and Saturday
• Bus: 60

The alchemical hermaphrodite fountain

The strangest piece on display in the *Museu Nacional de Arte Antiga* is, without a doubt, the *fonte bicéfala* (two-headed fountain), which the museum bought from a private owner in 1939.

Created in a 16th-century Lisbon workshop between 1501 and 1515, this limestone fountain was destined to supply the town with water. It is now the rarest municipal artefact in the museum's Portuguese sculpture collection. With a twisted column characteristic of Manueline style, this fountain brings together two crowned heads and two embossed coats of arms showing an armillary sphere and a fisherman's net, the respective symbols of Dom Manuel I and Dona Leonor, his third wife.

This work, whose origin and characteristic anthropomorphic representation continue to mystify art historians, holds significant symbolic meaning. The snake-like scales decorating the twisted column are a clear allusion to water, an element guarded by this reptile and which was controlled by the king, who ensured its fair distribution.

In Portugal, the 16th century was a period of contrasts – modernism and conservatism, innovation and tradition – characterised in Manueline art. Although, on the one hand, works from this period illustrate the persistence of medieval models, on the other they portray Franco-Italian innovations that, in sculpture, arrived in Portugal either through the direct importation of works or through the Iberian and French master-builders who sojourned in the country.

In this work, the union of the *fisherman's net* and the *armillary sphere* is very rare (the only other example can be seen at Pelourinho de Óbidos). It is an unequivocal symbol of the marriage between Dona Leonor of Austria and Dom Manuel I of Portugal.

As for the *serpent*, it is an ancient symbol of the earth, due to its slithering nature, but also of the primitive waters of the Ocean. It thus also represents the source of life for all the creatures of the Earth.

Dom Manuel I was a staunch supporter of hermetic philosophy, which was very fashionable at the time. So this work probably also symbolises the *Rebis* (or *Alchemical Hermaphrodite*), which represents the union of opposites that is necessary for man's spiritual fulfilment.

THE SYMBOLS OF CARVALHO MONTEIRO'S VAULT ❹

Cemitério dos Prazeres
Praça São João Bosco
• Open daily from 10am to 5pm
• Bus: 9, 18

> *The vault of the founder of Sintra's Quinta da Regaleira*

Located at No. 1382 of alley 11 (on the left) of the *Cemitério dos Prazeres* (Cemetery of Pleasures), this family mausoleum was built for António Augusto de Carvalho Monteiro (Rio de Janeiro, 27 November 1848 – Sintra, 25 October 1920), whose coffin was laid to rest here on 2 April 1922.

A wealthy trader with degrees in law and philosophy, António Carvalho Monteiro was a highly cultured man, as is notably illustrated by his Quinta da Regaleira, the monumental palace he had built at Sintra between 1900 and 1910. Here, on the vault, one finds the same post-Romantic and neo-Manueline tendencies as well as the mark of the Templar Seal that characterised his ideas of an Initiation to Portugality. He quenched his thirst for knowledge in the theosophical and hermetic writings of the prophet Bandarra, Dante's mythologies and especially the Portuguese prophecies and myths of Camões (see page 71).

Carvalho Monteiro turned to architect Luigi Manini to design this symbolically rich vault made from Carrara marble. It is composed of three parts, the first of which shows the Archangel Michael, guardian of souls, who represents the heavens and the world above. On the door to the upper vault,

a bee on an hourglass represents the passage of the human soul. The crypt, the underground lair of the immortals, is in the lower vault.

On either side of the vault façade stand traditional statues representing *Faith* holding a cross and *Hope* holding a chalice. Whereas *Hope* is bare-headed, the head of *Faith* is covered, thus illustrating that *Faith* is intimate, based solely on one's personal beliefs, while *Hope* is its supreme and ultimate affirmation.

THE KNIGHTS TEMPLAR: MYTH AND REALITY

The Order of the Poor Knights of Christ and of the Temple of Solomon (*Pauperes Commilitiones Christi Temlpoque Salomonici*) — more commonly known as the Order of the Templars or the Order of the Temple — was the most famous religious-military Order of the Middle Ages. Founded on returning from the First Crusade (1096) with the declared purpose of protecting Christian pilgrims to the Holy Land, the Order would exist for more than two centuries.

Officially recognised by Pope Honorius II in January 1128, the Order of the Temple quickly became the most highly regarded charitable order in Christendom, growing rapidly in both numbers and power. Distinguished by a white robe (revealing that members followed the Cistercian Rule of Cluny) bearing a red cross *pattée* (with serifs, see page 178), they formed the elite fighting force of the Crusades. The non-combatant members of the Order ran a vast financial empire extending throughout Christendom (even inventing the letter of credit, which was the first step towards the modern banking system). Ultimately, the Knights Templar had forts and churches throughout Europe and the Holy Land.

This magnificent organisational structure had a double goal: the formation of what would today be called a United States of Europe, and the provision of free and obligatory education (in keeping with the principles of the Templars themselves). Thus, the Order became established at two levels: one was outwardly visible to the whole world; the other was a more inward, esoteric existence. The 'secular' arm, as it were, comprised dynamic men of action and soldiers, while the esoteric arm was made up of the Order's true elite: the wise men and priests who formed the 'rearguard' to a body of knights and warriors. The two groups answered solely to the Grand Master of the Order and not to any king or pope. It was this which led to them being suspected of heresy, even if all they were doing was observing a rule of obedience. Similarly, the secrecy surrounding the Templars' ceremonies caused people to imagine that they engaged in heretic worship — something which was never proved because "civilians never enter into the houses of the military". The Order adhered rigorously to Apostolic Catholicism, even if some of its members had an intellectual interest in other cultures and theologies, and Gnosticism in particular. Gnostic symbols are sometimes to be found in the churches and castles the Templars built.

The spiritual mentor of the Order, Saint Bernard of Clairvaux, had initially selected nine members of its elite to go to Jerusalem, where King Baldwin III would allow them to establish their premises in the underground stables beneath the ruins of the Temple of Solomon. Certain traditions have it that they supposedly discovered the Cup of Solomon there, which had been hidden or lost since the time of Jesus Christ (the famous Holy Grail, see p. 20). The Templars are believed to have brought this Grail to the West, which from that point onwards extended its dominion over the whole world, just as the Order itself grew to dazzling heights.

With the loss of the Holy Land, the support the Templars enjoyed from Europe's monarchs began to wane. The French king, Philippe IV, who had no way of paying off a substantial debt to the Order, would begin to put pressure on Pope Clement V to take measures against the Templars. Evidence was forged and rumours spread, both with regard to sexual practices and religious unorthodoxy. It was said, for example, that the Templars worshipped a bizarre demonic figure called *Baphomet*, of which little was ever known exactly – except that it was a figure of pure invention (see page 227). Finally, in 1307, a large number of Templars in France were arrested and tortured until they made false confessions. They were then burnt at the stake or sentenced to service on the galleys. Philippe IV continued to pressure Pope Clement V, who finally dissolved the Order on 22 March 1312.

In Portugal, however, the king, Dom Dinis, considered the Templars to be innocent and afforded immediate protection to the sizeable number who had fled there from France. After the dissolution of the Order, the king immediately founded another that incorporated the old Templars: the Military Order of the Knights of Christ, also known as the Order of Christ. The abrupt disappearance of most of the "infrastructure" created in Europe by the Order of the Temple would give rise to a number of more or less extravagant legends and suppositions.

THE DUKE OF PALMELA'S MASONIC VAULT

Cemitério dos Prazeres
Praça São João Bosco
• Open daily from 10am to 5pm
• Bus: 9, 18

Europe's largest private funerary monument

The Duque de Palmela family vault, built in 1849, stands out prominently in the *Cemitério dos Prazeres* (Cemetery of Pleasures), as it is the largest private funerary monument in Europe.

It has belonged to Lisbon Municipal Council since 1997, when it was donated by engineer Manuel de Sousa Holstein Beck, the 4th Count of Póvoa. Its imposing dimensions, clear Masonic influences, and exceptional works of art (such as Canova's cenotaph and the tomb of the Teixeira Lopes brothers) make a visit worthwhile.

This mausoleum, which holds the bodies of 200 members of the Palmela family and their household staff, is the reproduction of a temple in the form of an ancient Egyptian pyramid. Inside, several statues by well-known sculptors adorn the tombs.

Its construction was ordered by the 1st Duke of Palmela, Pedro de Sousa Holstein (Turin 1781 – Lisbon 1850), a Portuguese politician and military man with liberal ideas. Although he was not a member, he sympathised with the esoteric ideals of symbolic Freemasonry and entrusted the mausoleum project to architect José Cinatti, a well-known Freemason.

In Freemasonry, 7, 5 and 3 are considered perfect numbers. Thus 7 steps must be climbed to enter the vault, then 5 more to reach the crypt. The number 3, which represents the Trinity, is found in the front triangle of the pyramid, behind the mausoleum's Greek porch entrance. At its top is a sculpture of the Angel of Good Death holding a cross and a closed book, attributed to Calmels.

The vault layout was designed after Solomon's Temple, in which beginners and apprentices sat around the north pillar, also called the Feminine or Lunar (*Bohaz*) pillar, while the initiates and companions sat around the south pillar, or the Masculine or Solar (*Jakin*) pillar. Here, the female servants are buried on the left (the north side), and the male servants on the right (the south side). Inside the chapel, on the east side, lies the Palmela family, thus representing the master initiates. Solomon's Temple is believed to have been paved with black and white stones, and here, too, the entrance to the mausoleum is laid with square stones of the same colour.

FONTE SANTA DOS PRAZERES **6**

Rua Coronel Ribeiro Viana
• Bus: 18

> **The miraculous waters of a legendary fountain**

At the turn in rua Coronel Ribeiro Viana in the *Cemitério dos Prazeres* (Cemetery of Pleasures), between numbers 11-D and 13, you will find the *Fonte Santa dos Prazeres* (Holy Fountain of Pleasures), almost hidden between modern buildings that have completely transformed the local landscape.

This fountain, after which this location is named, consists of a smooth, ochre-coloured back panel that has a lintel of white marble stretching across the entire width of the base. The basin that lies under the lintel is still the original, but has been restored several times. Inside, you can see a stone block where jars were placed and that still shows the marks of the iron supports. On the backplate, which ends in a cross, is a carved stone dating from the 16th century representing a boat whose prow forms a snake's head. It was placed there in 1835 during restoration work.

The water flowing from the fountain, from a spring-loaded metal tap, no longer comes from the spring that once fed it and that was said to heal the sick. The spring, which supposedly dried up due to the construction of the neighbouring buildings, was replaced by water from the EPAL network (Lisbon Water Supply company).

According to legend, well before 1599, a statue of the *Senhora dos Prazeres* (Our Lady of Pleasures) appeared over the spring, thus bestowing its water with virtuous healing powers. The Lisbon Senate consequently decided to have the tank and basin built, and to affix a gargoyle with the town's coat of arms there. The statue was later placed in a chapel built for it, but which no longer exists.

The chapel was sited on land named after its patron, the Quinta dos Prazeres, which is now used as the cemetery. Many people attended the chapel's Sunday services, especially those on the Sunday and Monday after Easter week because all of the religious brotherhoods, priests and monks of the Santos parish walked in procession, with crosses raised, singing a solemn mass. The chapel would have stood just above the *Fonte Santa*, in what is now rua Coronel Ribeiro Viana, before Travessa dos Prazeres, at No. 27.

The *Fonte Santa*'s snake ship and the name "Our Lady of Pleasures" evoke the concept of happiness in the afterlife through a *holy water* ritual healing both body and soul.

EPIC OF THE HOLY CONSTABLE RELICS ❼

Igreja de Santo Condestável
Campo de Ourique
• Open during mass at 9am and 6pm
• Tram: 28

> **He was a great prince, but he made himself a humble monk**

I n 1768, the bones of Dom Nuno that had survived the catastrophic 1755 earthquake were placed in a wooden copy of his coffin. They remained there until 1856 when they were removed and eventually placed in a velvet-lined urn in 1895. In 1912, the relics were placed in a silver reliquary and taken on a devotional pilgrimage around the country. Finally, they were stolen in 1967 and have never been recovered. Other bones, which had prudently been kept elsewhere, replaced the stolen ones. Some of these are venerated in the Terceira Order chapel at Largo do Carmo, while the rest are kept under the main altar at Santo Condestável church in Campo de Ourique.

The 1755 earthquake entirely destroyed the Carmo and Trindade neighbourhoods, which are still linked today in the famous saying *cair o Carmo e a Trindade* (knock down the Carmel and the Trinity). The Carmelite convent that Dom Nuno Álvares Pereira (1360-1431) had founded was razed to the ground and his tomb was lost. All that is left today are a few bones. Although his original tomb was a simple one, as he had requested, a more stately tomb was later constructed upon which was inscribed the following epitaph:

"Here lies that famous Nuno, the Constable, founder of the House of Bragança, excellent general, blessed monk, who during his life on earth so ardently desired the Kingdom of Heaven that after his death, he merited the eternal company of the Saints. His worldly honours were countless, but he turned his back on them. He was a great prince, but he made himself a humble monk. He founded, built and endowed this church in which his body rests."

The tomb was located near the main altar and contained a single shroud-enveloped body. A sort of insulated drawer protected the head to keep it from touching the dirt and lime. This custom, which had fallen out of practice a century before Dom Nuno Álvares Pereira's death, was the same used by the legendary knights of the Round Table that had so inspired Dom Nuno since his childhood (see p. 166). Indeed, his mother, Dona Íria, had nicknamed him the little *Galaaz*, or Galahad, after the purest of the knights. People sometimes smashed the church floor in order to take a handful of holy earth from his miraculous grave. They considered him to be the last medieval knight, a model of justice and perfection.

NUNO ÁLVARES PEREIRA, THE MIRACULOUS 14TH-CENTURY WARRIOR CANONISED IN 2009

Also known as the Holy Constable, Nuno Álvares Pereira (born 26 June 1360 in Cernache de Bonjardim, Sertã; died 1 April 1431 at the convent of Carmo, Lisbon) was a noble Portuguese knight of the 14th century who played a fundamental role in the 1383-1385 crisis, when Portugal fought against Castile for its independence. He was also the 2nd Count of Arraiolos, the 7th Count of Barcelos, the 3rd Count of Ourém, and attained the rank of Constable in the Portuguese army, a position equivalent to what today would be the Minister of Defence. At his death, he had already acquired his saintly reputation.

The son of Dom Álvaro Gonçalves Pereira, prior of the Order of Malta that was headquartered in the monastery at Flor da Rosa, in Crato, and of the noble-born Dona Íria Gonçalves do Carvalhal, Nuno Álvares Pereira grew up in his parent's home in Flor da Rosa. He learned the military arts and to enjoy reading, especially chivalrous stories in which "purity was the virtue that made the heroes of the Round Table invincible", and where it was possible for "one's soul and body to remain immaculate". He dreamed, telling his mother that one day he would also be a Grail Knight, that he was going to find the Grail and place it on the altar of the Lusitanian homeland. From then on, his mother called him "my little *Galahad*", after the hero who, according to the Round Table legend, succeeded in finding the Chalice. *Galahad* was also the nickname of Christ himself.

At the age of 13, Pereira entered the court of Ferdinand I and was made a knight with armour loaned by Dom João, Master of the Order of Avis. On 15 August 1376, at the age of 16, he married Dona Leonor Alvim at Vila Nova da Rainha in Azambuja. They had a daughter, Beatriz, but Dona Leonor died soon after giving birth (1388). Years later, on 1 November 1401, Beatriz married Dom Afonso, the bastard son of Dom João I and the 1st Duke of Bragança, at Paço de Frielas in Loures.

In 1383, when King Dom Fernando I died with princess Dona Beatriz (wife of King Dom João I of Castile) as his only heir, Dom Nuno Álvares was one of the first to support Dom João, Master of the Order of Avis, in his claim for the crown. Although he was the illegitimate son of Dom Pedro I of Portugal, crowning Dom João was preferable to losing the country's independence to the Castilians. After Dom Nuno Álvares' first military victory against the Castilians at the battle of Atoleiros in April 1384, Dom João of Avis named him Constable of Portugal and Count of Ourém.

On 6 April 1385, the Master of the Order of Avis was proclaimed King of Portugal at Coimbra. It did not take long for the Castilians to retaliate, as their powerful army soon invaded the country. On 14 August of the same year, the Portuguese forces confronted the Castilians at Aljubarrota. Despite their large disadvantage in terms of numbers (one Portuguese warrior to ten Castilians), the Portuguese won their stunning victory in less than an hour, thanks to the military genius of the Constable, who thus became, from then on, the patron saint of the Portuguese army.

The battle of Aljubarrota definitively marked the end of the country's political instability and reinforced its independence. On 25 July 1415, Dom Nuno Álvares Pereira set off with a fleet on expedition to Ceuta, in North Africa. It was his last battle. He later distributed his wealth to his family and the Carmelite Order (see p. 124) and became a mendicant monk at the Convent of the Carmelites in Lisbon. He had already earned his reputation as a saint, yet he kept his warrior soul.

It is said that, when Ceuta ran the risk of being retaken by the Moors, the old, stooped warrior wanted to go to the rescue. When others tried to dissuade him, he grabbed a lance and threw it from the convent's balcony. The lance crossed the valley below and pierced a door on the other side of Rossio. Dom Nuno declared, "If it were necessary, I could throw it all the way to Africa!" This is the source of the Portuguese expression "to throw a lance to Africa", meaning to overcome a great difficulty.

On 30 March 1431, a Good Friday, the "Holy Brother," as he was called, fell gravely ill. He died at noon on 1 April, Easter Sunday, at the age of 70.

The Portuguese people mourned their Holy Warrior. When they visit the *Holy Constable*, as he is still known today, visitors take a handful of soil from his tomb. The *Carmelite Chronicle* says that this miraculous soil, mixed with water and swallowed, has produced 12 resurrections, healed 24 paralysed people, 21 blind people, 21 deaf and dumb people, 18 people suffering from internal diseases, 16 people suffering from fatal diseases, 10 people with

fever and bleeding, and led to 6 apparitions of the Grand Knight in holy grace.

The miracles attributed to Nuno Alvares led Pope Benedict XV to beatify him on 23 January 1918, attributing the feast day of 6 November to him. At 9:33am, on 26 April 2009, Pope Benedict XVI canonised him as Saint Nuno of Santa Maria.

LION OF THE STAR   ❽

Jardim da Estrela
Bus: 20

F ounded in 1842-43, the *Jardim Guerra Junqueiro*, better known as the *Jardim da Estrela*, is one of the most beautiful and best-kept in Lisbon. It is known for the famous *Leão da Estrela* (Lion of the Star), which is also the name of a 1947 Portuguese

Remembering a lion from Mozambique

film. A few old-timers might remember what the garden's main point of interest was several decades ago – a magnificent specimen of the king of animals.

The nearly forgotten story of the famous *Leão da Estrela*, which became the star of 19th-century Lisbon society, is a wonderful episode of the city's unusual past. The animal was brought back from the Mozambique jungle by explorer Inacio de Paiva Raposo and was put on display here in 1869. Although a pair of lions was originally captured, only the male survived the voyage to Lisbon. He was named "Panhel", after the place of his capture, but he became known under the names of the "King of the Desert" and especially "Leão da Estrela", after the garden where he was kept. In April 1869, while his cage was being built, curious visitors were already hurrying to the garden asking about the lion, but he was being temporarily held on a property in Campo Pequeno. Finally, on 4 May 1869, a group of Galician workers transported the lion in a small cage from Campo Pequeno to Estrela, a difficult journey that took seven hours. The lion's permanent cage was very large and had two compartments, one in which he was on show to the public during the day, and the other, more private, where he slept at night.

Crowds formed immediately, as nine to ten thousand visitors are estimated to have come on the afternoon of 17 May 1869 alone. A few accidents occurred due to visitors who were more foolish and excited than the poor imprisoned animal that placidly contemplated the human spectacle.

Years later, the *Leão da Estrela* died of illness and old age. The last physical reminder of his presence disappeared at the end of the 1920s when his long-deserted cage was dismantled. The cage used to stand near the Pedro Alvares Cabral avenue gate, erected in 1941.

NB: The statue of Neptune and the lion was already in the garden before the other's arrival.

BELEM - SANTO AMARO - AJUDA

SÃO JERÓNIMO CHAPEL

Avenida Torre de Belém
• Open for visits on Wednesdays by reservation at the educational offices
of Jerónimos monastery
• Tel: 21 362 00 34
• Bus: 43

The forgotten chapel of Boitaca

The chapel of São Jerónimo (Saint Jerome) is located in a beautiful garden at the upper end of the grounds of Santa Maria de Belém monastery, a site that provides one of the finest panoramic views of the river and part of the city.

Designed by Frenchman Diogo de Boytac (Boitaca), the architect of the Jerónimos monastery's first phase, the chapel's construction was begun in 1514 and was completed in 1517 through the work of the Portuguese master Rodrigo Afonso. The chapel's design is a square with sides measuring roughly 11 metres. Six Renaissance-style gargoyles stand out on the smooth walls, and a small cross presides over the main façade. The upper part of the front door, which is very small, is decorated with Manueline armorial symbols – five coats of arms, a crown and armillary spheres.

A triumphal arch with multiple lobes and spikes on its pendentives and cable moulding stands inside the chapel. Above the keystone can be seen the coat of arms of Saint Jerome. The nave's vault is a fine architectural model, illustrating elegant craftsmanship and rich in decorations that are identical to those of the starred dome. Although the apse once had three altars covered in 15th-century Sevillian azulejos, the current structure dates from the 20th century, but still displays the original panels.

This chapel, where Pina Manique (1733-1805), the founder of the Casa Pia of Lisbon, was buried, is one of the three chapels that King Dom Manuel I had built in Belém at each end of the vast Jerónimos monastery grounds. The other two chapels are *Ermida de Nossa Senhora do Restelo* (Our Lady of Restelo), which was built during the time of crown prince Dom Henrique but has not survived to the present day, and *Santo Cristo*, near the "Os Belenenses" football stadium.

In a sense, these three chapels symbolised the Trinity: the chapel of Christ represented the Father; the chapel of Our Lady of Restelo, the Mother; and that of Saint Jerome, the Son.

MANUELINE ART: OF TRANSITION FROM DARKNESS TO LIGHT, OFTEN PRESENT IN DOOR AND WINDOW ORNAMENTATION

Manueline art, sometimes also called *Portuguese Late* or *Flamboyant Gothic*, is a style of architecture, sculpture and furniture developed in the 16th century during the reign of Dom Manuel I. It is a Portuguese variation of *Late Gothic* and *Lusitanian-Moorish* or *Mudejar art*, characterised by the systematic use of its own iconographic motifs, generally large in size to symbolise royal power. The term "Manueline" was coined by Francisco Adolfo Varnhagen in his work *Notícia Histórica e Descritiva do Mosteiro de Belém* [*History and Description of the Monastery of Belém*] in 1842.

At the time, this Manueline artistic trend was known as a Portuguese variation of *ad modum hispaniae* [Spanish-style] architecture, which itself was part of the *ao moderno* [modern] movement [later to be known as Late Gothic]. This architectural movement contrasted with *ancient style* or *Roman* architecture.

It was Frenchman Jean Boytac, leader of the Master Builders brotherhood, who officially introduced the Manueline style to Portugal, with his first attempts on the royal palace of Sintra and his masterpiece, the monumental Jerónimos (Hieronymite) monastery of Belém. Manueline style is above all a style of passage, of transition from darkness to light, which explains why it is predominantly found in the ornamentation of doors and windows. However, it does not hide the structure of the building, as superfluous ornamentation is avoided; the exterior and interior walls are generally left bare. Structural elements in areas of passage, such as columns, pillars, arches, friezes, oeils-de-boeuf and buttresses, as well as other elements such as tombs, fountains and religious monuments, are extensively decorated.

Manueline style, which is essentially a decorative art, is also characterised by the application of specific technical formulas regarding height, such as the multi-ribbed columns and vaults. It is precisely in sculpture that Manueline style reveals its greatest maturity and hegemony, because its decorative symbolism is recognised as a purely Portuguese style, and not as a variation of the style of other European countries. In this context, the sculptors and architects of Portugal inscribed a style of dynamic originality into the Portuguese artistic heritage, a style that astonishes still today.

The artistic "discourse" present in Manueline style was considerably influenced by the personality of King Dom Manuel I (1469-1521) as well as by his desire to organise a crusade that would unify the Western Christian world and Prester John's mythic Christian kingdom of the East (see p. 152). He would thus become the "King of the Seas" (a name some foreign authors in fact called him).

Manueline style principally transmits these messianic aspirations of a king whose accession to power was unusual, to say the least. He became king after the successive deaths of the other direct heirs to the throne (such as prince Dom Afonso and his brother Dom Diogo, who was assassinated). From the transposition of the *Spera Mundi*, the armillary sphere that became his symbol, to the interpretation of his own name, *Emmanuel* ("God with us" in Hebrew), numerous "signs" indicated that this king was God's "Elected One", chosen to accomplish great feats. His personal political view, influenced by his schoolmaster, Diogo Rebelo, and by the Joachistic tradition (Joachim of Fiore, see p. 188) that awaited the coming of the Messiah, led him to believe that he was destined to found a new world rule, a theme that would later be taken up by Father António Vieira under the name of the Quinto Império (Fifth Empire) (see p. 70).

THE SECRETS OF TORRE DE BELÉM

Praça do Império
• Open Tuesday to Sunday, 10am to 5pm (winter); 10am to 6:30pm (summer)
• Bus: 27

> *A winged bull, an acoustic phenomenon, a rhinoceros head ...*

A t the spot where Dom João II had chosen to have the Restelo ramparts built, on a small basaltic island of the Tagus about 180 metres from the right bank, King Dom Manuel I had built the *Castelo de São Vicente a par de Belém*, known today as the *Torre de Belém* (Bethlehem Tower). Designed by French architect Diogo Boitaca, its construction, which began around 1515 and was completed just before 1520, was overseen by Portuguese architect Francisco de Arruda. This edifice of magnificently dressed stone is considered to be one of the most beautiful examples of military architecture ever built.

It is not widely known that the Cross of Christ was featured here for the first time in its Greek version, which refers to the significance of the ecumenical mission of the Order of Christ to the Orient and explains the orientalism of Manueline art.

Winged bulls, the emblems of the vital force and virile strength that sentinels needed to confront potential enemies, support each refuge, with one exception. It is also interesting to note that the word bull (*boi* in Portuguese) is present in *Boitaca*, the name of the architect. The comfortable *king's hall*, where feasts and celebrations were held, has a curious acoustic phenomenon. If you whisper in one corner, your words can be distinctly heard in the opposite corner. Thus, people could not make whispered comments and hope to keep them a secret from the king or governor ...

The *chapel hall*, with its decorative motifs such as flames or masks (a symbol for time), has a black-and-white chequered floor at the middle of which is an enigmatic white octagon with a black square at its centre, a symbol of the local *mundus* of sacred geometry (see p. 202).

A rhinoceros head has been placed on the tower's northern façade in remembrance of the magnificent animal that the Sultan of Cambaia gave to Dom Manuel I. In 1517, a combat between the rhinoceros and an elephant was held on the beach in front of the tower, but without much success as the elephant ran away. The rhinoceros was then sent to Pope Leo X. King Francis I of France even came to admire it as it made its journey to Rome. Unfortunately, the rhinoceros died at sea. Its body was recovered, stuffed, and finally offered to its original addressee.

MEANING OF THE CROSS OF THE ORDER OF CHRIST

The Military Order of the Knights of Christ, commonly known as the Order of Christ, was founded in Portugal by King Dom Dinis on 15 March 1319. The universal heir of the disbanded Order of the Knights Templar, this order welcomed former Knights Templar and adopted the primitive cross, with some small changes.

Cross of the Order of Christ

Made famous by the Portuguese worldwide maritime diaspora and now the "ex-libris" of the national armorial symbols, the Cross of the Order of Christ is closely related to the traditional symbolism that accredits it with the same miraculous powers as the Templar Cross (which was attributed the majority of the miracles produced when it was invoked). The colours are the same (red to indicate the royal blood of Christ), as is the geometric schema.

The only notable difference is that the Templar Cross is Latin (or western) in accordance with the Bernardine rule (Saint Bernard of Clairvaux inspired the foundation of the Order of the Knights Templar), while that of the Order of Christ is Greek (or eastern) in accordance with the Benedictine rule that the order followed. The four ends of the Templar Cross, which are shaped like axe blades, evolved into a triangle shape in the Cross of Christ, in reference to the *Trinity*.

Templar Cross

The cross of the Order of Christ is based on an octagon (the number 8 symbolises perfection), as shown opposite. Note how the serifs* of the branches of the Greek cross form a 45° angle with the base, regardless of the length of the branches. The lines composing the design of the logo can be obtained by connecting the right angles at the top of each branch of the interior cross to the corners of the octagon.

The geometric composition of the Cross of Christ from the 14th to 16th centuries also complied with the proportion prescribed by the rule of Saint Benedict. The heroic deeds of Saint Benedict of Nursia (480-547) are generally taken from the work of his first biographer, Saint Gregory the Great. Leaving aside the countless seemingly supernatural events attributed to him to prove his saintliness, this saint possesses the characteristics of a veritable Initiate who knew how to impregnate each moment of his life with transcendence, making the most of the circumstances at hand. The fact that he is the patron saint of the Brothers of Christ indicates their thaumaturgic nature, in his image.

The *Rule of the Monasteries*, attributed to him, was the only rule capable of unifying the thousands of Christian trends practiced by the cenobites and hermits of Christianity's first millennium. The *Benedictine Rule*, which is quite similar to the *Latin Rule* of the Temple (both contain 73 chapters), shows the human value of emotional transcendence, where all the paths of Initiation are open, no particular path being able to dominate another. It also conserves the mystery of the primordial Tradition that is manifested in a hermetic form, whether by precise biblical quotations or in the precise and strict number of chapters it contains.

The rule of Saint Benedict also contains 73 chapters for numerological reasons, as 1+72 are numbers signifying the Unity integrated in a multiple group of 12 (12×6) as well as a Kabbalistic schema in which 70 corresponds to the Hebrew letter *ayin* (meaning "Divine Providence") and 2 to the letter *bet* (linked to the *sephirah Chokmah*, that of the *Messiah* — see p. 181).

*In typography, the *serifs* are the small lines or extensions placed at the ends of letters. In English, typefaces without *serifs* are called *sans-serif* (from the French *sans*, meaning without), and are also called *grotesques* (from the French *grotesque* and the German *grotesk*). The classification of typefaces as *serif* or *sans-serif* is the main division between them.

TRACES OF THE KABBALAH
ON JERÓNIMOS MONASTERY'S SOUTH GATE

❸

Monastery of Santa Maria de Belém
Praça do Império
• Opening times: Tuesday to Sunday, 10am to 5pm (October to April) and
10am to 6:30pm (May to September)
• Bus: 27, 49

Jerónimos and the Kabbalah

I n the esoteric Judaeo-Christian tradition, the *Kabbalah* is the way to understanding and man's spiritual realisation in God, by following a path in the Tree of Life, which is endowed with 10 divine attributes, called "spheres" or *sephirot* (see p. 183).

This tree, which represents the reciprocal path of communication between God and the community of man (the Church), is clearly depicted on the south gate of Jerónimos monastery. It evokes the presence of divine power in the human world.

At the lower end of the central vertical line is crown prince Henrique of Sagres (10), the Inspired One, who represents the community of man. At the opposite end is the Archangel Michael (1), God's emissary. The Virgin and Child (6) act as mediators between man and God.

Here, the relation between each of the 10 *sephirot* and their 10 corresponding figures on the gate are explained.

1. KETHER ELION (crown of God). At the top, where Archangel Michael, God's emissary, stands. Corresponds to *Metraton*, the intermediary between Heaven and Earth.

2. CHOKMAH (wisdom) and 3. BINAH (understanding). Correspond to the Fathers and Doctors of the Church.

4. CHESOD (mercy) and 5. GEBURAH (strength, fear). Correspond to the prophets and the Sybils or, in other words, the time before the coming of Christ.

6. TIPHARETH (beauty). At the centre of the image is the Virgem Nossa Senhora dos Reis Magos (Virgin Our Lady of the Magi).

7. NETZACH (victory, God's passive resistance) and 8. HOD (splendour, God's active force). Belong entirely to the ethic of the martyr and the evangelisation of Christ's apostles.

9. YESOD (foundation). Dominated by the young Saint Sebastian, the representation of the hidden soul (see Sebastianism, p. 134).

10. MALKUTH (kingdom). This *sephirah*, the kingdom of God on Earth, is represented by crown prince Dom Henrique, the Inspired One, who holds the privileged status of being the representative of the community of man before God. He also incarnates the feminine nature of the *Shekinah* (Holy Spirit). Henrique was a *momentary divine incarnation* and was at the origin of the early period of the great maritime discoveries.

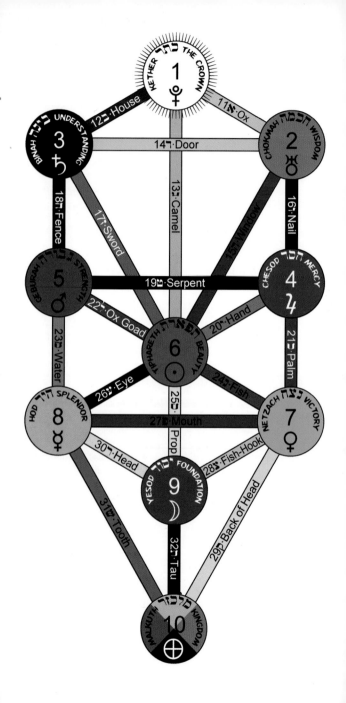

THE IBERIAN KABBALAH

The origin of the Kabbalah (*Tradition* in Hebrew) goes back to the dawn of time. After their flight from Egypt, led by Moses, the Hebrew people are believed to have inherited this secret, esoteric knowledge from Egyptian sages and to have adapted it to their monotheistic beliefs.

Since the Pharisees and the Sadducees had strayed from the correct understanding of the Pentateuch compiled in the Talmud, a new current of thought, that of the Essenes, appeared. They became the faithful keepers of the Kabbalah's wisdom until the arrival of Jesus Christ, who immediately incorporated it into his philosophy. After Christ, the Christian gnostics of Alexandria assimilated the Judaic Kabbalah to adapt it to their own concept of the universe and of man. The Judaeo-Christian Kabbalah was born.

In the 12th century, in his great work *Sepher ha-Zohar* (*Book of Splendour*), Rabbi Moses de León retranscribed the idea of the *Kabbalah*. Written in León but conceived in Lisbon, this work, along with the *Sepher ha-Yetzirah* (*Book of Creation*) dating from the 3rd century AD, forms the Kabbalistic system. Its origins go back to the *Maaseh Merkavah*, the first mystic Jewish system that interpreted the sacred texts of the Torah in the 1st century AD and created a new doctrine that, at first, was only transmitted orally (*shebeal pe*) by its followers (*iordei merkavah*).

In the *Sepher ha-Yetzirah*, which discusses the Universe and the laws that rule it, the patriarch Abraham reveals the understanding of Nature and its manifestations as emanations of God. The various levels of creation form ten interconnected spheres (*sephirot*) representing the paths of Kabbalistic spiritual realisation, which thus form the Tree of Life (*Otz Chaim*). The Spirit becoming the Word or Gospel is the first sphere and the breath that results from it, the second. The breath, by combining letters, gives birth to the other spheres. The third is that of water, which produces the Earth and matter. The fourth sphere is that of fire, which nourishes life. The last six spheres correspond to the four cardinal directions and the two poles.

Contrary to the *Rabbinical Kabbalah* attributed to Isaac Luria, a Jerusalem native, the Iberian Sephardim practised *Prophetic Kabbalah*. Attributed to Abraham Abulafia (AD 1200), *Prophetic Kabbalah* is at the origin of Spanish millenarianism,* Portuguese Sebastianism,** and other Luso-European gnostic currents of thought, such as the 16th-century Master Builders and Portuguese Freemasonry at the dawn of the 19th century.

*Spanish millenarianism: an apocalyptic doctrine about the End of Time and the coming of the universal Messiah.
**Portuguese Sebastianism: an apocalyptic doctrine about the coming of the Messiah as the king of Portugal.

DOM HENRIQUE: AN INITIATE WHO USED THE TREASURE OF THE TEMPLARS TO FINANCE GREAT DISCOVERIES

The son of King João I and Queen Dona Filipa de Lancaster, crown prince Dom Henrique of Burgundy and Lancaster was born in Porto in 1394 and lived in Viseu and Tomar for many years. It was in the Algarve, during a memorable voyage to Lagos and Sagres, that he developed his project of maritime expansion, the effects of which are still felt today. He died on 13 November 1460 and his body was transported to Santa Maria de Lagos church, which, at the time, was the seat of the *Confraria do Compromisso* (Brotherhood of Commitment). Over a month later, in 1461, on the orders of his uncle, King Dom Afonso V, the prince's mortal remains were transferred to the Santa Maria da Vitória monastery, generally known as Batalha. Diogo Gomes, a nobleman who had been present at the prince's death, told of the event and affirmed that Dom Henrique's body had not suffered any physical alterations, nearly two months after his death.

An imposing figure in Portuguese history "enlightened by the Holy Spirit, born and raised in divine mystery", according to his chronicler Gomes Eanes de Zurara (1410-1474), crown prince Dom Henrique of Burgundy (Henry the Navigator) was indisputably the mastermind and grand architect of what would later be called the maritime epic of the "Gesta Henriquina".

He incarnates the spiritual prerogatives of the Holy Spirit, or in other words the Third Person of the Holy Trinity called *Shiva* or *Siva* in the East, the anagram of *Avis*, the dynasty of which he was the most illustrious representative.

Dom Henrique was the supreme and secret master of the mysterious, but sovereign, Order of Mariz (*Allath-Maridj*), the eighth Grand Master and administrator of the Military Order of the Knights of Christ, and the founder of the British Order of the Garter in the city of Tomar, which served as a model to the British Order of Cardo, both of which had Saint George as patron. As for Dom Henrique, he chose the Divine Holy Spirit as his patron saint.

We have Dom Henrique to thank for the Hebrew translation of the book *Segredo dos Segredos de Astrologia* (*Secret of the Secrets of Astrology*), a treatise based on Aristotelian philosophy but that also explained Kabbalistic astrology. The book was heavily consulted by the sailors of the Naval Academy of Sagres. Indeed, it was thanks to their knowledge of astrology and astronomy, based on the position of the stars, that they traced their maritime routes.

The final administrator of the purported "Treasure of the Temple", Dom Henrique used wealth inherited from the former Knights Templar to finance the great discoveries. He was also a great academic, carrying out profound reforms of the University of Lisbon. To the disciplines that already existed at the beginning of the 15th century (Law – Decrees – Grammar – Logic – Physics – Philosophy – Theology – Music), Dom Henrique added Medicine, Natural and Moral Philosophy, Arithmetic, Geometry and Astrology in 1431. Zurara, the biographer of crown prince Henrique of Sagres, was an educated man with an interest in the occult sciences of the Kabbalah and in astrology, as his chronicles prove. The likeliness of his being a "New Christian" (converted Jew) is revealed in his *Chronicle of the Discovery and Conquest of Guinea*, in which he examined the horoscope of the illustrious prince and wrote: "However, I want to tell you here how, yet again because of a natural influence, this honoured Prince had an interest for all these [esoteric] things. And that because he was an Aries ascendant, which is in the house of *Mars*, and the exaltation of the *Sun*. Given that the aforementioned *Mars* was in Aquarius, which is in the house of Saturn, and in the house of Hope, that meant that this Lord strived towards heroic and strong conquests, in particular to search for things that were hidden from other men, and secretive, according to the quality of Saturn, in whose house he is. And because he is accompanied by the Sun, as I said, and the Sun is in the house of Jupiter, that meant that all these treaties and conquests would be carried out loyally, and with the pleasure of your King and Lord."

SYMBOLS OF THE CELL DOORS OF HIERONYMITE MONKS

❹

Santa Maria de Belém monastery
Praço do Império
• Opening times: Tuesday to Sunday, 10am to 5pm (October to April) and 10am to 6pm (May to September)
• Bus: 27

The Hieronymites and Joachim of Fiore's three ages of the world

T he cells of the monks of the Order of Saint Jerome, or the Hieronymites (Jerónimos), of the Santa Maria de Belém Monastery were connected to the cloister and to the interior of the church. Striking symbols on the doors of these cramped rooms can still be seen today.

The Hieronymite religious order, founded in Italy in 1377, is an evolution of the movement led by Tommasucio da Duccio (a member of the Third Order of Saint Francis of Assisi in his earlier days) towards the inspired spirituality of the *Fathers of the Desert*, to which Saint Jerome belonged.

The spirituality of the monks of the order was centred on *mental prayers* on Christ's wisdom, as Saint Jerome had practised. The Hieronymites followed the messianic and millenarian theories of the *Fraticelli* Franciscans, inspired by Joachim of Fiore, the author of the three ages of the world concept (see following double page). The last of these three ages, that of the Holy Spirit, was represented by *Emmanuel*, with whom Dom Manuel I shared his name, which partly explains why he offered this monastery to the Hieronymites who, as a result, came from Penha Longa de Sintra to settle here.

A sculpted *Janus* or *Tricephalous Christ* can be found on one of the cells. It symbolises the three ages of the world: the Past for the Father and Adam (associated with Jerusalem); the Present for the Son and Christ (Rome); and the Future for the Holy Spirit and Saint Benedict (Joachim of Fiore was a Cistercian, and thus also Benedictine) (Lisbon).

This concept is repeated in other compositions such as that of the three dogs, representing the guardians of the universal Church (*domini-canes*, dogs of the Lord or, in other words, the guardians of *traditional Wisdom*), or that of the three principles of alchemy: *Sulphur*, for the Spirit and the Father (an eagle on a Moor's head); *Mercury*, for the Soul and the Son (a head crowned with two angels, symbols of the winged androgyne); and *Salt*, for the Body and the Holy Spirit (a winged dragon with a three-horned baphometic head) (see p. 227). *Silver* is represented by a crowned queen and *Gold* by the crowned Mercury.

Etymologically, Jerónimo or *Hierónimo* comes from *Hiero-Manas*, meaning "inspired Spirit" or "universal Wisdom".

JOACHIM OF FIORE AND THE THREE AGES OF THE WORLD

Joachim of Fiore (Gioacchino da Fiore) was born in Celico, Cosenza in Calabra province, Italy, around 1132, and died in 1202 in the small abbey of San Martino de Canele, in Calabra. His remains were transferred to the abbey of San Giovanni in Fiore.

The son of Maurus of Celico, a notary in the service of the Norman kings of Sicily, Joachim grew up at court, but his religious vocation led him on a pilgrimage to the Holy Land to deepen his faith, which was prey to an intense mysticism. Legend says that, during Lent, while in contemplation before Mount Tabor, he had a vision and received the divine inspiration that would guide him all his life.

Back in Italy, he became a Benedictine monk at the abbey of Corazzo and was ordained a priest. He thus consecrated his time exclusively to biblical study, searching for the profound meaning of the Holy Scriptures. Because of his reputation for virtue and wisdom, he was elected to become abbot, but he sought an exemption from Pope Lucius III who freed him from his functions in 1182 so he could concentrate on his research.

In the following years, he worked on his books at the abbey of Casamari, assisted by Luca Campano, a young monk who would later become the archbishop of Cosenza. Increasingly focused on his work, Joachim of Fiore withdrew to the hermitage of Pietralata and founded Fiore Abbey in the Calabrian mountains. This abbey became the centre of a new independent order, nevertheless based on the Benedictine rule and statutes of the Cistercian order, but with more rigour and mysticism. The followers of this new order were called the *Joaquimitas* or *Florians*, in honour of its founder.

At his death, Fiore's saintly reputation led him to be venerated as such, even though he was never officially beatified. During his lifetime, he was considered to be a "prophetic, inspired" man.

The revolutionary character of his apocalyptic and prophetic thought mainly targeted the reform of the Church, for which he could count on wide support. It is rather surprising, in fact, that many Florian ideas that were condemned by the Lateran Council of 1215 were implicitly accepted by the Franciscans and eminent members of the clergy, even if they denounced the worldly and capitalistic aspects in which they participated. The thinking of Joachim of Fiore is expressed in three principle works: *Psalterium decem chordarum* (Psaltery of Ten Strings), *Liber concordie Novi ac Veteris Testamenti* (Book of Harmony of the New and Old Testaments) and *Expositio in Apocalypsim* (Exposition of the Apocalypse).

He wrote about the history of humanity (diverging from time to time with calculations and analogies to events recounted in the Old Testament), identified the connections to the New Testament, and divided history into three distinct ages: 1) the age of the Father, which begins with Adam and ends with Christ, making a total of 1260 years recounted in the Old

Testament; 2) the age of the Son, also lasting about 1260 years (which was meant to allow mystics to later adapt the date of the beginning of the Third Age) and described in the New Testament; and 3) the age of the Holy Spirit, which begins with the defeat of the antichrist, and whose sacred text, the *Eternal Gospel*, would be the fusion of the two previous texts (Old and New Testaments) leading to a period of universal Brotherhood in which Christians, Jews and Arabs would live in peace in a spiritualised atmosphere. It would be the quintessential Age of monks (priests), but the secular would not be excluded. Each age was to last 40 generations and be announced by a precursor. Osias had been the precursor of the second age begun by Zachary, father of John the Baptist. Saint Benedict was the precursor of the third age. The first age was the age of subservience, characterised by fear, and that of marriage (the married priests of the Old Testament). The second was the age of filial obedience, characterised by faith, and that of the priesthood. The third would be the age of liberty, characterised by charity, and that of monasticism. The *Eternal Gospel* is supposedly the book mentioned by Saint John in Revelation 14:6: "Then I saw another angel flying in the midst of heaven, having the everlasting gospel to preach to those who dwell on the earth, to every nation, tribe, tongue, and people."

With this brief summary it is possible to imagine the impact that Joachim of Fiore's ideas had on his followers. Later, the Franciscans adopted them and were quickly won over to the representatives of the Third Age, of which Saint Francis of Assisi became the herald. His ideas rapidly spread to southern Italy, from Sicily to Provence (where they appeared in the *Lais d'amour* and the *Romance of the Rose*, in the part written by Jean de Meug), to Aragon (through Arnado de Vilanova and Raimundo Lúlio) and to Portugal (by the Holy Roman Empress Isabelle). Later, the influence of the idea of the Coming is clearly seen in the religious orthodoxy of the Jesuits. It was at this time that the inspired thought of the Jesuit

Vera IOACCHIN Præclari est quã cernnis imago
'Qui vult, atque animo mirus in orbe fuit.

António Vieira appeared. He added two additional ages to those of Fiore, one linked to Sebastian the King and another to Sebastian the Saint. This coincides, in fact, with the hidden meaning of the *Veltro* of Dante's *Divine Comedy*. The Veltro, which Papini considers as the symbol of the Holy Spirit (*Veltro de Dio*), has its origin in Joachim of Fiore's *Eternal Gospel* and refers to the Clergy or the Papacy, as well as to the Crown or Throne, renovated by the Holy Spirit to inaugurate the new era of universal Peace and Liberty.

ALCHEMY AND THE RELIGIOUS ORDERS OF THE MIDDLE AGES AND THE RENAISSANCE

Most religious orders of the Middle Ages and the Renaissance considered *Alchemy* (from the Coptic term *Allah-Chemia*, or divine chemistry) as the *Art of the Holy Spirit* or *Royal Art* of the divine creation of the world and man. It was connected to Orthodox Catholic doctrine.

The followers of this Art divided it into two principal forms. *Spiritual alchemy* exclusively concerns the Inspiration of the soul, transforming the impure elements of the body in the refined states of spiritual consciousness, which is also called the *Way of the Repentants*. *Laboratory alchemy*, called the *Way of the Philosophers*, reproduces the alchemical universe of the transmutation of nature's impure elements into noble metals, such as silver and gold, in the laboratory. These two alchemical practices are generally followed in combination, thus becoming the *Way of the Humble*, where the humility is that of man faced with the grandeur of the universe reproduced in the laboratory (in Latin *labor + oratorium*); the alchemy of the (interior) soul is expressed exteriorly in the laboratory. Those who practice *Laboratory alchemy* with the sole purpose of finding silver and gold, and thus neglect the essential aspects of the betterment of the Soul, will fail and become *charlatans*, who might have a wide-ranging culture but certainly not the required moral qualities. To avoid becoming a *charlatan* (it was this heretic form that was condemned by the Church), followers must balance the heart and soul, culture and moral qualities, penitence and humility, to become a true philosopher.

The alchemy tradition has left a number of traces in Portugal, such as at the Convento de Cristo in Tomar where *Espagíria*, the fabrication of natural elixirs or medicines to help the needy, was practised. This practice was also carried out at the Convento dos Capuchos da Serra de Sintra and the Convento de São Diniz de Odivelas, where Dona Feliciana de Milão (1642-1705) wrote her *Discourse on the Philosopher's Stone*. At Lisbon's Convento do Carmo the decorated tomb of an alchemist surrounded by the instruments of his art can also be seen (see p. 167).

Ancient documents show that several alchemists passed through Lisbon, including Raimuno Lúlio, Arnaldo de Vilanova and Paracelse. Some Portuguese alchemists became known as early as the 13th century, such as *Pedro Hispano* (the only Portuguese pope, John XXI) who corresponded with *Albert the Great* and his disciple, *Thomas Aquinas*, who wrote the only alchemical treatise on water, *Tractatus Mirabilis Aquarium*. In the 15th century, King Dom Afonso V of Portugal wrote a treatise on the Philosopher's Stone in two parts: *Lapis Philosophorum* and *Divisão dos quatro elementos* (Division of the Four Elements). In 1556, the Inquisition accused Father António de Gouveia, a native of the Azores, of practicing alchemy and of knowing how to transform lead into gold. Monk Frei Vicente Nogueira saw his entire library of alchemical texts burnt to the ground by the Inquisition.

In the 17th century, the Portuguese mathematician Pedro Nunes corresponded with English alchemist John Dee, and Duarte Madeira Arrais wrote the alchemical treatise *Novae Philosophiae*. In the 18th century, King Dom João V encouraged the publication of the alchemical works of Raphael Bluteau, deservedly nicknamed the "Lusitanian Hermes". Anselmo Caetano Munhoz de Abreu e Castelo Branco also published his famous work dedicated to Dom João V, *Ennoea ou Aplicação do Entendimento sobre a Pedra Filosofal* (*Application of Knowledge on the Philosopher's Stone*). In 1724, a book of alchemical images, without any captions, also known as a *liber mutus*, or mute book, was published; it belonged to the library of King Dom Carlos. Finally, towards the end of the 19th century and during the first quarter of the 20th century, the Portuguese-Brazilian António Augusto Carvalho Monteiro suddenly appeared, leaving his property *Quinta da Regaleira* in Sintra. This is currently the largest building in Portugal containing alchemical elements associated with the Catholic gnosis. This unique site is thus a veritable *Roseiral Mariano* (philosophers' rose garden), the name given by the ancients to alchemical treatises, regardless of their form, whether written, drawn, painted or sculpted.

CHÃO SALGADO

Beco do Chão Salgado
Belém

> **Reminder of the scandal caused by a faked assassination attempt**

Behind the famous "Pastéis de Belém" bakery is the *Beco do Chão Salgado* (Salted Earth Alley), a place that most Lisbon residents have forgotten about but that is linked to a terrible event of Portuguese history that shocked all of civilised Europe in the 18th century.

As part of the conservative nobility and traditional clergy, represented by the Jesuits, were opposed to his social reforms, the marquis of Pombal tried to neutralise them. It is said that he went so far as to fake an assassination of King Dom José I on 3 September 1758, and to accuse the Távora family of the crime. This family, which was closely linked to the Jesuits, constituted the main opposition to the enlightened despot. The attack took place not far from here, near the palace of Dom José de Mascarenhas, duke of Aveiro, which was quite opportune as he was the most distinguished member of the Távora family.

Although the Távora family denied all accusations, they were condemned to death, their possessions were confiscated by the Crown, their name was erased from noble lineage and their familial coat of arms smashed to pieces. From that point on, it was forbidden to mention their name. The sentence ordered the execution of the entire family, women and children included.

The intervention of Queen Mariana and Dona Maria Francisca, heir to the throne, finally saved most of the family, to the great annoyance of the marquis of Pombal. As for the marquise of Távora, she was not spared. Along with the four other family members accused and sentenced to death, she was tortured and executed in public on 13 January 1759, nearby in front of what is now the palace of the president of the Republic. The execution reached unheard-of degrees of savagery. The bones of the hands and feet of the condemned, who were decapitated, were broken with clubs, and the rest of the bodies were burned and their ashes thrown in the Tagus. Making the most of the occasion, the event was used to throw the Jesuits out of the kingdom.

The duke of Aveiro's palace was also demolished and salt was poured on the ground, a punishment ordered by the marquis of Pombal so that nothing would ever grow there again. Yet the same year, Dom José I had a stone monument to the family erected. It displays five sculpted rings, one for each executed member of the Távora family. At its base, a funerary stele recounts the event.

RESTOS MORTAIS
DE SEBASTIÃO JOSE DE CARVALHO E MELLO
1º MARQUEZ DE POMBAL
N. 13·V·1699   M. 8·V·1782

THE TOMB OF THE MARQUIS OF POMBAL

Igreja da Senhora do Livramento e São José
Largo da Memória, Freguesia da Ajuda
• Opening times: Monday to Saturday, 3pm to 7pm
• Visit by reservation. Tel: 213635295
• Bus: 27, 29

> **The posthumous adventures of the marquis of Pombal**

The mortal remains of Sebastião José de Carvalho e Mello, the famous and controversial marquis of Pombal (see p. 209), are in Ajuda, in an urn kept in the church of the Senhora do Livramento e São José (Our Lady of Deliverance and Saint Joseph). This neoclassical Lisbon monument was built in 1760, two years after the Távora family episode (see p. 193). King Dom José I had it built to commemorate the fact that he escaped the assassination attempt carried out against him at this spot. It is now known as the *Igreja da Memória* (Memory church).

Sebastião José passed away in Pombal and was initially buried on 8 May 1782, dressed in his Franciscan habit and the insignias of the Order of Christ, in the church of the São Francisco de Nossa Senhora do Cardel convent. During the third French invasion of Portugal (1807), the convent was used as a barracks and the tomb was desecrated by soldiers hoping to find valuable objects. Despite the intervention of general Massena, the soldiers left the bones on the church floor. In 1856, marshal Saldanha ordered the transfer of the remains to Lisbon, while the empty coffin remained as a "relic" in Pombal.

The mortal remains of the marquis of Pombal were placed in an abandoned tomb reposing on four carved elephants in the *Mercês* (Graces) chapel, on rua do Século (Century), where he had been baptised on 6 June 1699. When the decision was made to demolish this chapel in the 20th century, the tomb and remains were to be disposed of along with the rest of the sacristy, but on 7 November 1910, Lisbon's Municipal Board added them to its archives. It was not until 1923 that they were transferred to this church of Memory, on the initiative of the fifth marquis of Pombal and a Republican commission presided over by Borges Grainha, a Freemason.

The church was closed until 23 December 1951, when a group of soldiers from the 7th Cavalry Regiment reopened it for worship on their own initiative. It had to be closed again in 1985 when lightning seriously damaged its dome.

Thanks to recent renovations, the church and the marquis of Pombal's mausoleum is now open to the public (advance booking required).

THE *POMPEIA* ROOM OF PALÁCIO DA EGA   ❼

Freguesia de Alcântara
Calçada da Boa-Hora, 30
• Free guided tour by reservation
Instituto de Investigaçao Científica Tropical
• Tel: 213616330
• Bus: 203

Hidden behind Ega Moniz hospital, the *Pátio do Saldanha* palace, better known as *Palácio da Ega*, contains part of Lisbon's lost history. To visit this splendid 16th-century palace, take the calçada da Boa-Hora (Right-Time road), where the Overseas Historic Archives are now located.

Forgotten marvels

Surrounded by a beautiful garden embellished with a large lake, the building bears the coat of arms of the Coutinho, Albuquerque and Saldanha families on its central gate.

Inside is the magnificent *Pompeia* room, dating from the beginning of the 18th century, also called the "music room", "column room" or "room of the marshals". Especially notable are the statue of the god of music, the magnificent columns, the dome, and the frescoes on the walls, as well as the eight 18th-century azulejo panels depicting Europe's main ports, the work of Dutch artist Boumeester.

The room's current design dates from the 19th century, when it was entirely remodelled. The original wooden ceiling was removed, the upper windows were filled in, and a false dome resting on eight hollow wooden columns was constructed. The panels were also repainted in the style of the period, leaving the original azulejos untouched.

The most famous resident and owner of this palace was the countess of Ega, Dona Juliana Maria Luisa Carolina Sofia de Oyenhausen e Almeida, who, in 1795, wed the second count of Ega (the name of a village near Coimbra), Aires José Maria de Saldanha. The countess was a very beautiful woman and had several famous lovers, including general Junot and marshal Beresford.

THE ORIGIN OF *STROGANOFF*

After the count's death, the countess of Ega remarried. Her new husband was the count of Stroganoff, a Russian from Saint Petersburg, the city where she would die in 1827. During her time there, she discovered a recipe from the count's chef that later became famous in Portugal. By browning beef, tomatoes and mushrooms in a casserole, then adding sour cream, it is easy to make *Stroganoff*, to be served with rice.

THE ROTUNDA OF SANTO AMARO CHAPEL ⑧

Alto de Santo Amaro
• Open Saturday and Sunday during mass (9am and 7pm)
• Bus: 751

When in danger of drowning ... The stunning Saint Maurus chapel (Santo Amaro), founded in 1549, is located in Alto de Santo Amaro de Alcântara, on a hill with a superb view of part of the city and the Tagus. The legend depicted on the polychrome azulejo panels that cover the interior tells of a Galician ship on the verge of being wrecked. The crew cried out to Saint Maurus, praying to be saved, and the ship was miraculously able to reach the shore at this part of the river. To thank Heaven, they founded this chapel.

Another, more plausible, version says that the chapel was founded by 14 monks of the Ordem de Cristo (Order of Christ) after their return from Rome, where they had gone in pilgrimage to the basilica of Saint John Lateran. When their boat passed by on the Tagus, they noticed this spot and chose it as the place where they would dedicate their lives to asceticism. On 15 January 1532, they founded the Brotherhood of Saint Maurus, the saint to evoke when in danger of drowning.

The brotherhood received numerous honours and privileges from the pope and different Portuguese kings. Connected to Saint John Lateran, the brotherhood was made up exclusively of nobles, such as the Count of Sabugosa, who was still its clerk when it was abolished in 1836. The feasts of 15 January, in honour of Saint Maurus, were celebrated enthusiastically and were full of life and colour thanks to the participation of the Galicians, the traditional water-carriers of Lisbon.

This circular chapel has a rather curious polygonal layout, with seven straight sides, four of which are closed while the other three are open and thus form the doors to the church, also circular in form. This creates a sort of "ambulatory" (charola or rotunda) like that found in the Freires de Cristo convent at Tomar, which is itself inspired by the octagonal design of the São Gregório Nazianzeno chapel of Santa Maria do Olival located in the same city.

A section of the azulejo panels near the side altar depicts Saint Maurus, dressed as a pilgrim, leaning on a rod and carrying the Book of Hours. This saint, abbot and bishop is the champion of those suffering from broken arms or legs because, when he was alive, he had the miraculous power of healing broken bones. This was perhaps also an allusion to his missionary work, in the sense that he rectified deviations to the original doctrine just as he realigned bones. This explains why the ambulatory is decorated with arm and leg motifs, also found on the azulejos of the step leading to the main altar.

WHO WAS SAINT MAURUS?

Maurus of Glanfeuil (feast day 15 January) is believed to have been born in Rome in AD 510 and to have died in Glanfeuil (Anjou) in 584. Along with Saint Benedict of Nursia – of whom he was the closest disciple – he is believed to have founded the abbey of Monte Cassino (Italy) in 528. He introduced the Order of Saint Benedict to Gaul by founding the Glanfeuil monastery, where he taught agriculture to peasants. As a result, he is the patron saint of farmers to this day. In the 17'th century, his name was given to a reformed Benedictine congregation. Among his numerous miracles, one of the best known is when he saved a fellow monk, Placidus, who was drowning in Subiaco lake with no one nearby to save him. Saint Benedict had a vision of this danger and ordered Saint Maurus to go and save the young monk. He walked on the water, took hold of his fellow monk by the hair, and saved him from imminent death.

Saint Maurus is also venerated because he heals arthritic and rheumatic pains, as well as headaches. Iconographically, he is shown wearing a monk's hood and holding an crozier and a crutch.

MYSTERY OF THE AMBULATORY OF THE KNIGHTS TEMPLAR

It is fairly certain that the Order of Christ built the ambulatory of the Santo Amaro d'Alcântara hermitage with the purpose of reproducing west of Lisbon the Great Ambulatory (*Grande Charola*) that it had built in Tomar.

Dom Gualdim Pais, the master of the Portuguese Templars, commissioned the construction of the Tomar convent ambulatory from the Builder-Monks of the Cistercian Order on 1 March 1160. It was to be the exact replica of the Mosque of Omar and the Church of the Holy Sepulchre, two round constructions on the site of the ancient Temple of Solomon in Jerusalem. The purpose of building the Tomar ambulatory was to create a new Temple of Jerusalem at the head of the Iberian peninsula to synthesise the West and the traditionalism of the East. The three religions of the Book (Judaism, Christianity and Islam) would thus be united in a single Temple, that of the true, unique God, in concordance with the theory of the transfer of power (*translatio imperii*).

Originally, the oratory of the Knights Templar stood here. Based on the classic form of Syrian mosques, it was a very simple construction. However, in 1356, when Tomar became the seat of the Order of Christ (on the suppression of the Knights Templar), prince Dom Henrique (see p. 184) had the ambulatory modified and enhanced in order to adapt it to the functions of the new convent of the Order of Christ and to make it the apse

of the Order's church. Most of the paintings and frescoes (almost exclusively biblical scenes) date from the 16th century, as do the golden statues below the Byzantine dome.

The interior of the ambulatory is octagonal in shape (the centre has eight sides), while the exterior walls are composed of – or, more precisely, were once composed of – sixteen sides reinforced by solid buttresses (two side sections were removed when the church was enlarged in the 16th century during the Manueline period).

In this drawing of the ambulatory, or *charola* — a word that reflects its circular form, like the related French term *carole*, meaning a circle, or dance in the round (as in *rotunda*, another word for a round building) — we find the *octagon* and the number *eight* reflected in the number of sides. The medieval symbolism of both is fully adapted to the original functions of the oratory and the apse of the ambulatory. Considered as the place of passage from mortality to immortality, it served as a psychopomp (guide of souls) or as the intermediary between the two worlds, the visible and the invisible, and hence represented the Arch of the Alliance of God and Humanity.

In the Middle Ages, the *octagon* was the intermediary shape between the square (the Earth) and the circle (the Heavens) and was the spiritual symbol of passage, that is of Christ's resurrection and of the beginning of human perfection. The octagon thus expresses Divine Power in the mortal world, represented by the manifestation of Heavenly Jerusalem on Earth, in this case the ambulatory.

The Kabbalistic meaning of the number *eight* further reinforces the symbolic significance of the octagon as it holds the double square of the Earth and of Man in balance. In the Christian tradition, the number *eight* is the number of Redemption and Prosperity. Eight is also one more than seven, or, in other words, one more than Plenitude. Christ exceeded the Jewish Plenitude (the number seven) in his resurrection on the dawn of the eighth day. The eighth day became the first day (the day of the Lord, *Dominica dies*), Sunday, in opposition to Saturday (*Shabbat*), or rest, the seventh day when the Lord rested after his Work of Creation. This is why the most important Christian celebrations (Easter and Christmas) last eight days. They are celebrated for eight days, with the second Sunday being the extension of the celebration. The eighth day, the day of the Resurrection, connects Christians, through baptism, to the paschal mystery of Jesus Christ (the octagonal form is often found in the design of baptismal fonts). In Roman art, the eight-pointed star (one square superposed over another at an angle, a symbol of spiritual transformation) and the eight-petalled rosette have the same significance.

THE FIVE BASIC SOLIDS AND SACRED GEOMETRY

Sacred geometry is a world vision according to which the basic criteria for existence are perceived as being *sacred*. Through them can be contemplated the *Magnum Misterium*, the Universal *Grand Project*, by learning its laws, principles and the inter-relationships of shapes. These universal shapes are systematised in a geometric complex in which each figure has its own mathematical and philosophical interpretation. They are applied in projects of *sacred architecture* and *sacred art*, which always use the "divine" proportions in which Man reflects the Universe, and vice versa. It is a common belief that *sacred geometry* and its mathematical relationships, which are harmonic and proportional, are also found in Music, Light and Cosmology. Man first discovered this system of values in prehistoric times, in the megalithic and Neolithic cultures, for example, and some consider it to be a universal facet of the human condition.

Sacred geometry is fundamental to the construction of sacred structures, such as synagogues, churches and mosques, and also plays a role in creating the interior sacred space of temples, through the altars and tabernacles. Passed down from Graeco-Egyptian culture and exported to ancient Rome, *sacred geometry* in the European Middle Ages inspired the creation of the Roman and Gothic architecture of Europe's medieval cathedrals, which incorporate this geometry of sacred symbolism.

It is said that Pythagoras (Samos, *c.* 570 BC – Metapontum, *c.* 497 BC) was the one who founded the system of *sacred geometry* in his school in

Croton, Greece. This Greek philosopher and mathematician is believed to have brought the knowledge he acquired in Egypt and India back to Greece. Using the golden ratio (1.618) and applying it to the geometric forms of the five basic solids, Pythagoras created the mathematical method universally known as *Pythagorean geometry*.

To create the five solids (the tetrahedron or pyramid, the hexahedron or cube, the octahedron, the dodecahedron and the icosahedron), about which Plato would later philosophise (to such a point that they would become known as the *five Platonic solids*), Pythagoras was inspired by the Greek myth about the child-god Dionysus' toys: a basket, dice, top, ball and mirror. On a cosmic level, the *basket* represents the Universe; the dice, the *five Platonic solids* symbolising the natural elements (ether, air, fire, water, earth); the *top* is the atom of matter; the *ball*, the Earth's globe; and, finally, the *mirror* reflects the work of the Supreme Geometrist (*Dionysus*), which itself is the universal manifestation of Life and Consciousness, of God towards Man and vice versa. Each of the five Platonic solids also represents a planetary energy that is connected by its form to a natural element. Thus, the *dodecahedron* is traditionally linked to Venus and ether, the natural quintessence, expressed by a temple's dome. The *octahedron*, linked to Saturn and the air, represents the transept's cross. The *tetrahedron*, linked to Mars and fire, is symbolised by the openings in the temple through which light gushes forth. The *icosahedron*, linked to the Moon and water, establishes the harmony of forms in the temple *design*, constructing the connecting lines between the altars and columns. Finally, the *hexahedron* (cube), fixes the Sun to its element, the earth, by determining the shape of the temple's foundation or floor.

The main purpose of *sacred geometry* is thus to create Universal Perfection through perfect mathematical forms and calculations, and, by using *sacred architecture*, to connect the Multiple to the Single in a space that is geometrically dedicated to this end.

FARTHER AWAY

THE ANDALUZ FOUNTAIN BAS-RELIEF

Largo do Andaluz
• Metro: Picoas

Lisbon's oldest coat of arms

On the Andaluz fountain, the discreet inscription dating from 1336 of a boat with two ravens, one on the prow and the other on the stern, is the oldest representation of the city of Lisbon's coat of arms.

The ravens are connected with the legend of Saint Vincent (São Vicente), according to which the birds watched over the saint's corpse as angels took it by boat from the coast of Sagres, in the Algarve, to Lisbon. He died in 1173, during the reign of Dom Afonso Henriques (see opposite).

Legend also says that the boat was a ship of the Knights Templar with black and white sails and that it carried the coffin to Lisbon Cathedral (Sé Patriarcal). As for the ravens, they stayed in the cloisters (see p. 28). A few decades ago, visitors could still see the birds flying around the cathedral, but today they are kept in a cage in a corner of São Jorge castle. The relics of São Vicente belong to the Sé treasure (see photo).

Symbolically, ravens are the birds that hold Divine Wisdom. They see the past and the future, like *Huggin* and *Munnin* (Thought and Memory) the companions of the Norse god *Odin*, who, perched on his shoulders, caw secrets

about the past and the future into his ear. The same goes for the two Hindu gods *Kuvera* and *Mahima*.

The lowered sails and ropes also form a six-pointed star composed of two interlaced triangles, the symbol of the universal equilibrium of soul and body.

THE RAVEN: THE ORIGIN OF THE NAME "LISBON"?

The raven, a prophetic bird and messenger of the gods, totem of the Sun god *Lug*, was called *Lu* or *Li* in the Ligurian language (Genoese), which is the root of the name *Lisboa* or *Lusibona*, a derivative of *Ulisibona* and *Ulisipa*.

SAINT VINCENT, THE SAINT OF DIVINE WISDOM

Patron saint of Lisbon, Saint Vincent (São Vicente – Victorious One) is a Christian martyr from Valencia, Spain, where he was deacon. Martyred during the time of Roman emperor Diocletian (3rd century AD), he was burnt alive on a white-hot iron gate. According to legend, his corpse was then rolled up in ox-hide, attached to a millstone by the neck, and thrown into the sea. The tide took it all the way to the Algarve coast and deposited it on the cape that now bears his name, where a hermitage of Mozarabic Christians stood.

Some of the hermits noticed two enormous ravens flying around a corpse in the rocks. Upon closer inspection, they recognised the body of the martyr, which they immediately gathered up, with the birds looking on

closely. The saint's remains provoked numerous miracles and the site's saintly reputation increased to such an extent that it became nearly as famous as the Saint James of Compostela pilgrimage, which was rapidly developing at the time (8th century AD).

Later, King Afonso Henriques ordered that the saint's mortal remains be transported to Lisbon aboard a Templar ship. They let the tide guide the boat, still accompanied by the ravens, one at the stern and the other at the prow.

THE SYMBOLS OF SAINT VINCENT'S SEA VOYAGE

There is a great difference between steering a boat and letting it drift. Vincent, who knew the secrets of this tricky maritime route, knew how to drift, meaning that he placed himself in the hands of Providence in whom he had total confidence. He thus illustrated the wisdom worthy of someone who had received the Holy Spirit.

The detail that, according to legend, he came to Lisbon aboard a Templar ship, accompanied by symbolic ravens (see opposite), also attributes a special power to the Order of the Templars, thanks to their connection with the saint.

Finally, the *millstone*, the iconographic element of this saint, is in shape equivocal to a *wheel*. It is, however, impossible to move and turn without the very special *Initiation* that the force needed to accomplish this feat can provide.

SYMBOLS OF THE MARQUIS OF POMBAL STATUE

❷

Praça Marquês de Pombal
• Metro: Marquês de Pombal

Pombal, the true leader of Lusitanian Freemasonry

The Masonic influence of the statue of Sebastião José de Carvalho e Mello, Marquis de Pombal, is openly illustrated even in the low grille that surrounds the statue. On its wrought-iron panels can be seen an interlaced sceptre and torch, allegories of various social activities that the marquis strongly influenced by reforming and developing them (agriculture, fishing, industry, etc.) in order to enter a new era of progress.

On the architecture panel, the architect's instruments are depicted in their symbolic Masonic use. Thus you can see the "line of love" from which a triangle hangs. Attached to the triangle is a stonemason's hammer and, more importantly, the flaming torch of Knowledge intertwined with the sceptre of enlightened Absolutism that characterised the marquis's government.

It is unknown whether the marquis of Pombal was actually a Freemason, despite evidence that he may have been initiated in a lodge in London or in Vienna when he was the ambassador of Portugal in these cities. Whatever the case, he is the veritable leader of Lusitanian Freemasonry. Portuguese Freemasons paid him homage on his 100th and 200th anniversaries by transferring his ashes and building this monumental statue, financed by public subscription.

Dr Sebastião de Magalhães Lima (Rio de Janeiro 1850 – Lisbon 1928), a renowned Freemason and several times Grand Master of the Grand Orient Lusitano Unido, presided over the 1926 executive committee for the construction of this monument. Despite religious objections, this monument symbolising national unity under the aegis of a charismatic leader was finally accepted by the Republicans and by partisans of the New State.

MARQUIS OF POMBAL

Sebastião José de Carvalho e Mello, Marquis de Pombal and Count of Oeiras (Lisbon, 1699 – Leiria, 1782), held the position of Secretary of State (Prime Minister) of the kingdom of King Dom José I from 1750 to 1777.

A representative of this enlightened despotism, he experienced Portuguese history of the Enlightenment at first hand and played an important role in bringing Portugal closer to the more advanced countries of Central and Northern Europe, notably on an economic and social level.

In Portugal, he put an end to the *auto-da-fé* practices dating from the Holy Inquisition and to the segregation of New Christians (Jews forced to convert to Catholicism). He did not officially abolish the Portuguese Inquisition, however, which continued until 1821. He was also principally responsible for the expulsion of the Jesuits from Portugal and its colonies. His administration was marked by two famous difficulties. The challenge presented by the Lisbon earthquake of 1755 led to him being known in history books as the renovator of the city's architecture (according to hermetic principles – see p. 60). The *Távoras trial* was a political intrigue that had dramatic consequences (see p. 193).

Although his affiliation to the Ancient and Accepted Scottish Rite of Freemasonry cannot be specifically proven, it is nevertheless generally accepted that he had close ties to the *Casa Real dos Maçons da Lusitânia*, particularly through Carlos Mardel and Reinaldo dos Santos, as well as to the *Casa dos 24*.

CRUZEIRO
DO
SUL

PAVILHÃO CARLOS LOPES

Parque Eduardo VII
• Metro: Rotunda
• Visit by appointment. Tel: 21 354 15 28

*A moving
pavilion*

Sited on the western fringes of Eduardo VII park, the former *Liberdade* (Freedom) park and green area of the city, the *Pavilhão dos Desportos* (Sports Pavilion) is one of the Portuguese pavilions of the grand 1922 World's Fair in Rio de Janeiro, organised to commemorate the 100th anniversary of Brazil's independence.

Built in Portugal by architects Guilherme and Carlos Rebello de Andrade and Alfredo Assunção Santos, the structure was inaugurated on 21 May 1923, nine months after the official opening of the event. During the fair, the president of the Republic of Brazil, Dr Artur Bernardes, visited the pavilion, where one of the many exhibits was the Santa Cruz hydroplane Gago Coutinho and Sacadura Cabral used to cross the Atlantic from Lisbon to Rio de Janeiro.

Rebuilt at its current location in the Portuguese capital by a renowned team supervised by architect Jorge Segurado, it became the *Exhibition Hall* and reopened for the large Portuguese Industrial Exhibition on 3 October 1932.

In 1946, the pavilion was renovated to host the 1947 Roller Hockey World Championships, which was when it became known as the Sports Pavilion. Recently, on 27 August 1984, it was renamed after one of the key figures of Portuguese athletics, *Carlos Lopes.* Note especially the stairs, the azulejo panels and the statues, particularly the two framing the main portico representing *Science* and *Art*, the work of sculptor Raul Xavier in 1935.

The four azulejo panels decorating the exterior façade at the front of the building date from 1922 and are by painter Jorge Colaço. They depict four great events in Portuguese history: *Ourique* – the battle of Baixo Alentejo that led to the foundation of Portugal (see p. 102), when Dom Afonso Henriques, encouraged by a vision of Christ, defeated the seven Moorish kings; *A Ala dos Namorados* (Regiment of the Lovers) – a unit of very young men (hence their name) commanded by the Saint Constable Nuno Álvares Pereira that won renown at the Battle of Aljubarrota and guaranteed the nation's independence; *Sagres* – the name of the Nautical School in the Algarve, as an allusion to crown prince Dom Henrique and the period of maritime expansion; *Cruzeiro do sul* – (Southern Cross, the characteristic constellation of the Southern Hemisphere that served as a guide for sailors), a reference to Brazil, discovered in 1500 by Pedro Álvares Cabral.

CHURCH OF SÃO SEBASTIÃO DA PEDREIRA ❹

Tel: 21 354 54 70
• Metro: Pedreira

I n today's *São Sebastião da Pedreira* (Saint Sebastian of the Quarry) parish, on the square of the same name where the *estrada Real* (Royal way) to Sintra began, stands a church that was originally a chapel of the Saint Sebastian brotherhood, composed of artillerymen from the Lisbon garrison.

> *The relic of Saint Sebastian: the origins of the identification of saint with king*

Every time the city was contaminated by the plague, the population took refuge outside the city walls and the Mouraria (Moorish district) at this spot, significantly named *Bons Ares* (Good Air) in the 16th century. Its therapeutic waters, which flowed from a spring behind the chapel (now the fountain depicting a coat of arms), helped to protect the people from the ravages of the disease, as did their profound faith in the site's patron saint.

As time went by, this miraculous site, with its small chapel built over a quarry, took on the name *São Sebastião da Pedreira* and became famous as such.

It built such a reputation that, in 1527, Holy Roman Emperor Charles V sent a gift to his brother-in-law, Dom João III of Portugal – the precious relic of the arm of Saint Sebastian. Esteeming, after the fact, that the relic deserved a larger religious edifice as its home, he finally sent it to the Saint Vicente de Fora monastery where the holy martyr had been venerated since the reign of Dom Manuel I. The relic is still kept there. The current church, built over the early chapel, was inaugurated in 1652, during the reign of Dom João IV. Inside is the tomb of Dom João Bermudes, patriarch of Alexandria and Ethiopia, who died in 1570, and whose tomb comes from the original chapel. The walls are covered in large azulejo panels dating from 1718 and which allude to Saint Sebastian's life. On the ceiling, a central painting by João Câncio de Sousa dating from the end of the 19th century depicts the "Glory of Saint Sebastian". He is shown rising towards heaven surrounded by little angels and his wife (Irene) who pulls arrows from his body. It is remarkable that Sebastian, the recognised patron saint of the artillerymen of Lisbon, is also, in the traditional context, the perfect paradigm of the warrior caste or *Kshatriya* (as Saint Anthony is for the sacerdotal caste or *Brahmin*). This recalls the *King of the World* theory (see p. 105) that Dom Sebastião wanted to fulfil when he undertook a military campaign with disastrous results (see p. 101).

The *Saint Sebastian – King Sebastian* emulation began when the king wanted to build a church in the centre of Terreiro do Paço to house the relic first offered to the original chapel of Pedreira, but the project was never finished.

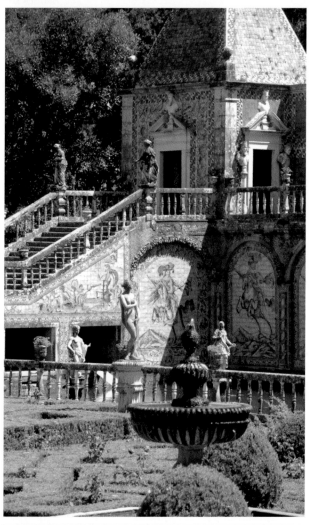

In the sublime *Galeria dos Reis* (Gallery of the Kings), the busts of twenty Portuguese monarchs are on display (the three Spanish kings of the Philippine dynasty who ruled Portugal during its occupation are absent) along with those of count Dom Henrique (father of Afonso Henriques), Dom Fernando (the prince-saint, son of Dom João I, who died in captivity in Africa), and the Holy Constable Nuno Álvares Pereira. They stand along a façade of fourteen large blind arches, the centre of which leads to a grotto where Mount Helicon can be seen with the winged horse Pegasus and the eleven Muses, which recall the symbolism of the "Isle of Love" evoked in the immortal Luís de Camões' *Lusiads*.

SYMBOLS OF THE PALÁCIO-MUSEU MARQUESES DE FRONTEIRA

⑤

Largo de São Domingos de Benfica, 1
• Opening times: Monday to Saturday, 10:30am to 12pm
• Bus: 72

N ow unfortunately surrounded by a desolate landscape of motorways and soulless buildings, the superb gardens

A hermetic garden

of the Palácio-Museu Marqueses de Fronteira were designed in the 17th century according to hermetic principles (see p. 60) in order to attract the celestial energies whose principal elements it reproduces.

The *Garden of Venus*, which opens onto the *Lake House* facing a lake where a chimerical figure pours water into a basin, suggests the presence of a pavilion dedicated to mysterious ancient cults, as was the fashion in Mannerist gardens. These gardens reproduce the garden of the goddess of Love (*Venus*) on the former site of a labyrinth whose centre is now occupied by the lake. At the centre of the lake, an ancient sculpture of a young child bearing a coiled snake symbolises the Quest of and Initiation to the Divine Love of troubadours and minstrels.

The *Varanda da Oratória* (Loggia of the Oratory) is composed of niches holding statues of the gods of the Graeco-Roman pantheon representing the planets. The walls of the niches have azulejo panels depicting allegorical female figures symbolising the seven liberal Arts and their respective attributes. This sculptural ensemble is organised as follows: Diana / Arithmetic – Mercury / Music – Venus / Dialectic – Apollo / Rhetoric – Mars / Poetry (replacing Geometry) – Jupiter / Astronomy – Saturn / Architecture.

The *Jardim Grande* (Grand Garden) is made up of a network of octagonal box-tree shrubs dividing four large flowerbeds which themselves are divided into four smaller ones. At the centre of the network lies a basin of water with a column surmounted by an armillary sphere. Four other smaller fountains and twelve lead statues (both masculine and feminine) stand at the corners of the flowerbeds. The low wall near the palace's east-facing façade is covered with polychrome azulejo panels on the themes of the four elements, the planets and the constellations, while the front wall is covered with panels depicting the mythological allegories of the twelve months of the year and their corresponding agricultural activities. The north wall, opposite the central basin, bears azulejos on the theme of the twelve signs of the zodiac.

Structured in this manner, the *Jardim Grande* represents the *Macrocosm* or the Universe, in complementary opposition to the *Microcosm*, Man, symbolised by the *Garden of Venus*. The meeting point of the two is found in the *Varanda da Oratória*, where Science is assisted by the gods and where Hermes (or Mercury) emerges as the link between the general evolution of Man in the Universe and of the Universe influenced by Man, thus justifying the hermetic axiom according to which "as it is above, so it is below" and vice-versa (see p. 60).

SYMBOLS OF THE ZOOLOGICAL GARDEN ❻

Open daily, 10am to 8pm
• Metro: Sete Rios
• Note: The rose garden is currently closed. It should reopen soon.

*Reproduction
of the mythical
Garden of Eden*

Considered one of the most beautiful gardens in the world, the *Jardim Zoológico da Aclimataçado de Lisboa* (Zoological Garden of Acclimatisation of Lisbon), inaugurated in 1905 at Quinta das Laranjeiras, Sete Rios, was originally an attempt to recreate the biblical Garden of Eden where humans and animals could coexist in peace. This zoo's project was apparently inspired by the *Garden of Delights* of biblical, Chaldean and Hindu accounts of paradise, where the four kingdoms of nature (mineral, vegetable, animal and human) come together in harmony. The mineral kingdom is represented by water and granite, the plant kingdom by the variety of flora, the animal kingdom by the zoological species presented, and the human kingdom by the visitors. The Freemasons and Rosicrucians that inspired the architecture of this exceptional site (the Count of Farrobo, Dom Fernando II and Dr António Carvalho Monteiro, among others) dispersed spiritual symbols throughout the garden to illustrate the different stages of the initiatory voyage. They thus recreated the Garden of the Gods in a recreational area that invites people to stroll and converse. Surrounded by hedges and pavilions at the heart of the garden, Lisbon's rose garden follows the style of French landscape artist Le Nôtre. A very pretty suspended bridge leads to the rose garden, an allegory of the passage to the superior world. At the top of each column of the bridge stands one of the four master Egyptian builders, the guardians of the four directions of the corners of the garden that, when regrouped in pairs, illustrate the *Principle of Polarity* that rules Universal Life (Spirit and Matter, Sun and Moon, Day and Night, North and South, etc.). The rose garden is like the garden of an open temple, with its fountains, hidden recesses, labyrinths, summits, granite spheres and wreaths, and mythological figures full of esoteric significance. The androgynous sphinxes (male face and female breasts) represent the perfect man, or the disciple that has reached his spiritual realisation. The Assyrian dragons illustrate the divine wisdom of the same disciple. The geese are an allusion to enlightened companionship and the dolphins a symbol of the philosopher's stone. The rose garden is planted in the centre of the cross of this enchanting, dream-like place and is a synthesis of the whole zoo.

The garden is also part of a spiritual path, or the "initiatory voyage" of the human conscience with the goal of attaining eternal wisdom. The path includes several edifices of this former *Quinta das Laranjeiras*: the Farrobo palace (Physical); the Tália theatre (Vital); the Farrobo garden (Emotional); and the rose garden (Mental). Together, the *Quinta* represents Eden (Spiritual).

TÁLIA THEATRE

❼

Estrada das Laranjeiras
• Metro: Laranjeiras

A long-forgotten theatre

Largely unknown, the *teatro Tália* is now owned by the state which is thus responsible for its restoration and preservation. Its abandoned ruins are located on estrada das Laranjeiras (Orange Tree way), in front of the former palace of count Farrobo, built in 1820.

Originally a rather rudimentary theatre, it was reconstructed in 1842 with gas lighting, a grand innovation for the period. The premiere of Almeida Garrett's *Frei Luís de Sousa* was played here and 18 operas were performed between 1834 and 1853.

King Dom Fernando II and Queen Dona Maria II were frequent visitors. At the death of the queen, of whom the count of Farrobo had been a great friend, the social and artistic life of the palace and theatre were put on hold. In 1856, theatrical activity began again with Italian operas and Portuguese and French comedies, but, on 9 September 1862, an accidental fire caused by worker negligence entirely destroyed the building. As the count of Farrobo's fortune had started to dwindle, the theatre was not rebuilt and was left in the state it can be seen in today.

With an audience capacity of 560, the *Tália* had luxurious boxes and an opulent ballroom with walls covered in sumptuous Venetian mirrors that reflected the lights of numerous chandeliers, producing a dazzling effect.

Thalia is one of the Greek Muses, the patron of comedy.

The theatre held a strong spiritual symbolism imparted by Joaquim Pedro de Quintela (1801-1869), second baron of Quintela and first count of Farrobo, who was a highly ranked Freemason. The building's exterior façade, reached by climbing four steps, is supported by four Tuscan columns fronted by the same number of Egyptian sphinxes. They symbolise the *theatre of initiation* entered into through the four-beat rhythm of the Earth (marked by the four seasons, the four phases of the Moon, etc.) and where everyone is the actor of their own evolution. At the top of the triangular pediment, a statue of Erato, the Muse of lyric poetry, holds her lyre in her right hand and rests it against her thigh.

THE HEAD OF DIOGO ALVES

Teatro Anatómico da Faculdade de Medicina de Lisboa
- Visit by appointment at the office of the School of Medicine
- Tel: 22 903 98 26
- Metro: Cidade Universitária

> **The head of this 19th-century Lisbon serial killer is kept in formaldehyde**

Diogo Alves, a Galician born at Santa Xertrudes de Samos, in Lugo, came to live in Lisbon at a very young age. Nicknamed *Pancadas*, he quickly became famous as the *assassin of the Águas Livres aqueduct*. From 1836 to 1839, he committed a series of ghastly crimes there at the instigation of his girlfriend, Gertrudes Maria, nicknamed *Parreirinha* and who was the owner of a tavern in Palhavã. After robbing his victims, he would throw them off the top of the aqueduct (65 metres high) at night to simulate a suicide. The authorities finally captured him in 1840, after he and his gang killed a doctor and his family during a burglary. Curiously, they were condemned to death by hanging for this crime, but not for the aqueduct murders, which were not even mentioned in the trial.

He carried one secret to the grave – how he had obtained duplicate keys to the aqueduct galleries where he would lie in wait before attacking and assassinating his victims. It was not until after he was imprisoned and the apparent suicides ended that they were discovered to be the work of the sinister Diogo Alves, who killed 76 people in the summer of 1837 alone.

Once the death sentence had been carried out at the Cais do Tojo, at 2:15pm on 19 February 1841, scientists at the Lisbon School of Medicine and Surgery were so intrigued by his criminality that they retrieved his head for study. It can still be seen today in the anatomy theatre of the School of Medicine, preserved in formaldehyde. His calm expression provides no hint of the man he truly was.

The crimes of serial killer Diogo Alves, the last person to be condemned to death in Portugal, became the subject of one of the country's first silent films in 1911. His romanticised biography, which made his story famous, was first published in 1877 and reprinted in 2006. In 2005, his head was part of the exhibit *Cem peças para o museu de Medicina* (One hundred pieces for the Museum of Medicine), organised by the Museu Nacional de Arte Antiga.

Small businessmen and travelling merchants of the area frequently took the *passeio dos Arcos* (promenade of the Arches), the entrance of the public path to the *aqueduto das Águas Livres* (aqueduct of the Free Waters). It was closed in 1844, however, following the killings of Diogo Alves.

THE "DIAPHANISED HAND" OF LISBON'S TEATRO ANATÓMICO

Teatro Anatómico da Faculdade de Medicina de Lisboa
• Visit by appointment at the office of the School of Medicine
• Tel. 22 903 98 26
• Metro: Cidade Universitária

> *A veritable little museum of horrors*

Lisbon's anatomy theatre exhibits a series of human specimens that can truly shock more sensitive visitors. This museum also possesses books and objects from the field of medico-legal surgery as well as a book dating from 1543 that the Lisbon School of Medicine inherited from the former School of Medicine and Surgery. Illustrated with detailed drawings of anatomical research and dissections, this book entitled *De humani corporis fabrica* by Andreas Vasalius (1514-1564) was for centuries the reference for medicine and anatomy in Portugal.

Besides all the teaching aids proposed by the museum, it also owns human organs preserved in various liquids, including the head of Diogo Alves preserved in formaldehyde (see preceding page).

One of the other spectacular pieces of the collection is a diaphanous hand, also preserved in a jar. The hand was made transparent, nearly invisible in fact, by a chemical injection that set, dehydrated and "diaphanised" the tissues. The hand was then submerged in paraffin. In addition to the hand, there are dehydrated and coloured lungs, almost in fragments, revealing their bronchial tubes and bronchioles sub-divided and separated.

Typical artefacts of Portuguese medicine are also exhibited. Of particular note are several instruments invented and used by Portuguese professor Egas Moniz (1875-1955), winner of the Nobel Prize for Medicine in 1949, including an example of a syringe, a pair of *leucótomos*, and an apparatus for carrying out lobotomies and cutting the nerve fibres connecting the prefrontal cortex to the rest of the brain. Also to be found is the first cerebral angiography, a technique developed by Egas Moniz that consists of injecting a contrasting agent into the blood to see the blood vessels inside the skull by radiography, thus facilitating the diagnosis of cerebral pathologies, notably tumours.

Portugal's contribution to science does not stop there. There is the apparatus that Reinaldo dos Santos (1880-1970) used for the first aortography, a negatoscope and numerous other instruments that have made medical history in Portugal.

MACHADA GROTTO

Igreja de Nossa Senhora da Luz
Largo da Luz, Carnide
• Visits to the grotto on request at the church office (10am to 12pm and 3pm to 6pm)
• Mass at 9am and 6pm
• Metro: Colégio Militar

> *A rainbow in a miraculous grotto*

A round 1437 or 1459, Pêro Martins, a Christian Templar knight, was being held prisoner by the Moors in Tangiers when Our Lady, infused with light, appeared to him. She promised he would soon be freed if, upon his release, he went to a place called Carnide in Lisbon and, at the spot where he would find her image in a grotto, built a chapel in her honour.

So it came pass. Pêro Martins, once freed, quickly began looking for the statue at the spot indicated by the Virgin and finally found it in a grotto from which emanated a radiant rainbow-like light. He named the site *Luz* (Light). From this cave flowed miraculous waters that poured into the *Fonte do Machado* or *da Machada*, mentioned in a document dated 27 May 1311, and which was named after the woman who was the beneficiary of Chelas, Urraca Martins Machado or Machada, a Cistercian nun of the São Bernardo monastery in Carnide.

The church of *Nossa Senhora da Luz* (Our Lady of the Light), to which the miraculous fountain and grotto were annexed, was thus inaugurated on 8 September 1464 for the celebration of the Nativity of the Virgin, one year after the statue was discovered. The altar stands directly over the fountain of holy water, as the church is built over the little cave.

To enter the grotto of Machada, which can be visited by request, you pass through the Manueline gate of the first chapel, which was a site of pilgrimage. Then the gallery opens to where water flows into a sunken basin under an arch, above which is the statue of the Virgin of the Light, the Holy Child at her bosom.

Inside the church, the central painting of the surprising altarpiece by Francisco Venegas (17th century) depicts the *Alegoria da Imaculada Conceiçao* (Allegory of the Immaculate Conception), one of the rare female nudes (a Venus) to have survived the Counter-Reformation.

TEMPLAR INSCRIPTIONS ⓫

Igreja de São João Baptista
Largo de São João Baptista, Lumiar
• Visits when open for mass, 9am and 5pm
• Metro: Ameixoeira

> ### *Is Brigid's skull linked to the Templars' Baphomet?*

Three largely unknown tombs are set in the lateral exterior wall of São João Baptista church in Lumiar. One of them bears this striking inscription: "In these tombs lie three Iberian knights who brought the head of Saint Brigid the Blessed of Hibernia (Ireland), whose relics are found in this chapel erected in her memory by the officers of this blessed Lady in January 1283."

As the church is on Ameixoeira land, which belonged to the Order of the Knights Templar, it is not impossible for these tombs to be those of Templar knights, who illustrate, here, the Iberian myth of the three sons of the goddess *Brigit* (*Brian*, *Iuchar* and *Uar*, the spirits of inspiration who, according to Celtic mythology, collectively fathered one son – *Ecne*, science or poetry).

Before becoming the Christian *Brigid*, she was the Celtic divinity *Brigit*, venerated throughout Western Europe. Her skull was brought here in 1283, on the order of the Provincial Grand Master of the Temple of Portugal, Dom Frei João Fernandes, who had close connections to king-troubadour Dom Dinis and wise king Dom Afonso de Leão e Castela.

Yet today, in the São João Bastista church of Lumiar, worshippers venerate the relic of Saint Brigid of Ireland that was supposedly brought from the monastery of São Dinis de Ovidela: a piece of her skull in an elegant urn of gilded silver in Dom João V style. For some, this skull is connected to the mythical *Baphomet* of the Knights Templar (see opposite).

WHAT EXACTLY IS THE BAPHOMET?

It is sometimes said that the Templars venerated a mysterious skull that transmitted oracles and supposedly dictated the so-called Secret Rule containing the most unimaginable blasphemies. This legend is evidently the fruit of the imagination of 19th-century Romantic writers, because there is no earlier proof of the existence of a satanic skull.

The word *Baphomet* itself did not exist in medieval vocabulary; the Church and the Templars did not know it. It was invented by Occitan troubadours who used it on very rare occasions in their poetic confabulations. Although the Templars may have had a skull relic (they were great collectors of sacred relics), it would not have had this meaning. Even if, for Catholicism, it principally represents death, the skull has a double meaning. As it holds the brain, it holds the highest and greatest part of man. It is thus the quintessentially sacred part of the body and the symbol of the discovery of Supreme Knowledge. The word *Baphomet* comes from the Arabic phrase *ouba-al-fometh*, meaning the "mouth of the Father", and in this sense is linked to the supreme knowledge that comes from the Father himself. As the Father contains the Son and the Holy Spirit, he is also the *Light of Wisdom* to which some gave the meaning, from late Greek, of *Baphêtmétous*. This is the meaning used in the poem *Ira et Dolor*, written in 1265 by an Occitan troubadour: "*E Baphomet obra de son poder*" ("And Baphomet made his power shine"). In the Moorish language of the Iberian Peninsula, inherited from the Muslims, it was written as *Abufihamat* (pronounced *Buphimat*) and signified "Father, Source, Understanding". An expression derived from it, *Ras-el-fah-mat*, means "Head of Knowledge" and refers to the mental capacity of a man who had reached a level of perfection of his conscience. This process is alluded to in the expression "I'm constructing a head", used by some Sufic schools of the Iberian Peninsula. The medieval Christians pejoratively called it *Bafometarias* and *Carvoarias* (coal-like), meaning "black and diabolical" in a popular sense. Indeed, secret knowledge was taught and practised in this tradition, which, for an ignorant Christian, could only be "things of the Devil".

The "baphometic" skull thus represents *mental illumination*, just like Brigit the Celt when she presided over the pagan festival of *Imbolc*, a feast of purification celebrating the end of winter, a symbol of the illumination of the world after the infertile darkness. That is why Saint Brigid is also sometimes represented carrying a candle with a cow at her feet, signifying lactation, in this case a reference to the renewal of life in spring.

SEPVLTVRA DE ANTONIO CAVIDE·
EDE SVA MVLHER D MARIANA ANTO
NIA DE CASTRO.

THE LIZARD OF PENHA DE FRANÇA

Igreja de Nossa Senhora da Penha
Largo da Penha de França
• Bus: 107

Nossa Senhora da Penha de França church serves as an important witness of supernatural interventions in Lisbon. Indeed, a curious collection of *ex-votos* exhibited in a *casa dos milagres* (house of miracles) can be found inside.

> *A lizard that saved the Lusitanians from paganism*

Among all the legends surrounding this site, the main one is undoubtedly that of the *lizard of Penha*. A first version tells of a tired pilgrim who was sleeping on the slope of the hill as an enormous lizard prepared to attack him. The pilgrim was awakened by Our Lady, who thus miraculously saved him. Another version says he was woken up by the lizard, who was sent by Our Lady to save him from a snake attack, the snake thus symbolising the ancient "pagan" religion of the Arabs, and the lizard the dragon of the Christian Lusitanians. Until 1739, a large stuffed lizard was kept in this church and was later replaced by a wooden version that was lost in the earthquake of 1755. The second version of the legend finally prevailed and today visitors can still see a carved wooden lizard and snake on the doors to the sacristy. The legend of the lizard is also depicted on the azulejo panel on the rear façade of the church.

The founding of the current Nossa Senhora da Penha convent by the order of the discalced monks of Saint Augustine dates from the end of the 16th century. Before, António Simões, a gilder of Lisbon who followed Dom Sebastião on the Alcácer-Quibir expedition (the greatest military disaster in Portuguese history), had had a modest chapel built here. He had made the vow to have nine different images of Our Lady made if he were to return save and sound. He kept his promise – the last image was called Nossa Senhora da Penha de França and was placed in the Vitória chapel. On a cold night in 1597, António Simões, who had not yet finished the chapel, raised the standard of Our Lady in front of the chapel. The painting then started to shine extraordinarily through the night. The news quickly spread and worship of the Virgin of Penha took root.

Legend says that it is in this steep place that *Ulysses* fell in love with the "snake-goddess" *Ofiússa*.

The name *Penha de França* has been kept in memory of a French monk who supposedly discovered a statue of the Virgin hidden in a rock, near where the church now stands, sometime during the Arab occupation of the Iberian Peninsula when Christianity was dominated by Islam.

FUNDADA

EM

1849

THE FORMER VIÚVA LAMEGO CERAMICS FACTORY

Largo do Intendente
• Metro: Intendente

> **A beautiful collection of azulejos in a run-down neighbourhood**

The former residence of chief of police Diogo Inácio de Pina Manique (1733-1805) stands in the middle of the avenue that bears his name. The austere nature of this multi-storey building contrasts with the neoclassical Pombaline style adopted during Lisbon's reconstruction after the earthquake of 1755.

Its sobriety perfectly suits its first owner, who took his authority as chief of police so seriously that he reprimanded anything that was not "moral and in accordance with good manners" with exaggerated zeal.

The building, located in what is now a run-down neighbourhood, is decorated from top to bottom with superb polychrome azulejo panels.

This former *fábrica de cerâmica Viúva Lamego* (Viúva Lamego ceramics factory) was founded by António da Costa Lamego, who owned the property after the police chief. He set up his ceramics factory in 1849. He had the building that can be seen today constructed and the façade on Largo do Intendente covered with azulejo panels in 1865. Earthenware and ceramic art pieces are still made here today.

Upon the death of its founder, the factory was renamed after his widow, *Viúva Lamego*, and passed into the hands of one of his sons, who then sold it to his brother-in-law, João Garcia Jerpe. João Agostinho da Costa Garcia later took it over.

With the construction of avenida de Dona Amélia (rebaptised Almirante Reis in 1911), the company lost its land next to the convento do Desterro (now a hospital), but this loss had a positive affect on the building, as its main façade now faces this avenue.

The facilities on Largo do Intendente Pina Manique are now uniquely dedicated to exhibitions and sales, the manufacturing side having been transferred to Palma de Baixo. Azulejos of excellent quality, both industrial and artistic, such as those designed by Vieira da Silva (some of which cover the Cidade Universitária metro station), are produced there. The company's headquarters are at Abrunheira.

THE *EX-VOTOS* AROUND THE STATUE OF DOCTOR SOUSA MARTINS

Campo Mártires da Pátria
• Bus: 30

14

> **The miraculous interventions of the "Father of the Poor"**

The number of *ex-votos* piled around the statue of Dr José Tomás de Sousa Martins (Alhandra, 7 March 1843 – Alhandra, 18 August 1897), in the centre of campo dos Mártires da Pátria, illustrates the adulation still felt for him. He has almost acquired the status of a secular *saint*. Still today, the miraculous intervention of Dr Sousa Martins is invoked for health problems.

His statue, the work of sculptor Costa Motta, was inaugurated on 7 April 1904, on the initiative of a committee formed by the friends of the lamented professor. With this sculpture, Casimiro José de Lima was determined to keep alive the memory of Sousa Martins, head of the School of Medicine.

A tenured professor with degrees in pharmacy and medicine, Sousa Martins was most known for his intense, and often unpaid, work in the fight against tuberculosis. Not in the least religious and a strong humanist, he was a brilliant speaker gifted with humour and intelligence, a man who was always full of generosity towards the most disadvantaged. He had a great influence on his colleagues, students and patients, an influence that spread to such a point that people started coming to his statue, as well as his tomb at the Alhandra cemetery, to adulate him.

His fight against tuberculosis meant that he was exposed to the disease through his daily direct contact with his patients. Many died holding his hand and some even claimed to see a strange aura around his head. He often told his students, "When you enter a hospital at night and you hear a sick patient moan, go to his bed and see what the poor patient needs, and if you don't have anything to give him, give him a smile."

His skills as a clinician and his humanist habit of not charging the most disadvantaged patients earned him the title of "Father of the Poor" as a

sign of recognition from those he treated. This sentiment grew even more following the tragic circumstances of his death. He committed suicide after learning that he, too, had contracted tuberculosis.

He killed himself at dawn on 18 August 1897, leaving these words: "Before snatching away a man's life, tuberculosis makes him endure a long martyrdom, and makes of the martyr an invalid."

SECRETS OF CASA DOS 24

Igreja de São José dos Carpinteiros
Rua de São José,. 64
• Visit by reservation. Tel. 218855230
• Near Freguesia de São José
• Metro: Restauradores

A "Masonic" church in Lisbon

L ess well-known today than it was during the Pombaline period, the church of *São José dos Carpinteiros* (Saint Joseph of the Carpenters) was originally called *São José de Entre as Hortas* (Saint Joseph among the Vegetable Gardens). In 1545, the Brothers of the Saint Joseph Patriarchate built a small chapel in the middle of the vegetable gardens that stretched north of the Santo Antão gates. It became a parish church in 1567.

The church was the seat of the São José dos Carpinteiros brotherhood, which had originated in the corporation of the masters of the *Casa dos 24* (House of 24) or *da Mesa* (of the Table). This corporation brought together the main trades of the city that gave their names to the streets of the Baixa district: *correeiros* (leather artisans), *sapateiros* (cobblers), *ourives* (silversmiths), among others. Founded during the reign of Dom João I (1357-1433) and abolished on 7 May 1834, the *Casa dos 24* corporation met here from 1750. All the documents relating to its operation and spending, from the 18th century onwards are still kept here, as are the brotherhood's original flag and the table they used for their meetings, which can be found in the chapel. This 17th-century table is made from tropical hardwood and has 24 drawers, one for each of its 24 seats. The São José dos Carpinteiros brotherhood, whose coat of arms (depicting the tree of paradise and the Freemason compass) is on the side door, began its activities in 1522 with masons and carpenters. Stonecutters, woodworkers and cabinet-makers joined later. Europe's oldest trade corporation, it probably inspired the speculative Freemasonry founded in France in 1717.

The church façade was destroyed in the earthquake of 1755, but was immediately reconstructed under the orders of master-mason Caetano Tomás. On each side of the entrance topped with an oval Saint Joseph medallion, you can see carved stones on which the temple's important dates are inscribed as well as, in relief, masonry and carpentry tools, the philosophical significations of which are found in the names of neighbouring streets: Faith, Hope and Love (Charity).

> The visionary and prophetic faith of these master tradesmen may have been identical to that of the discalced Augustine monks of Santo Antão o Velho who once had a convent here. Destroyed in the 1755 earthquake, it had become famous thanks to its abbot, Frei Maria da Visitação, who was condemned by the Inquisition for his controversial miracles and grandiose visions. However, these visions had brought him international renown, to the point that the duke of Medina Sidonia came to ask him to bless the standard of the *Invincible Armada*.

THE HERMETIC AZULEJOS OF MADRE DE DEUS

Museu Nacional do Azulejo
Rua da Madre Deus, 4
• Open Tuesday, 2pm to 6pm, and Wednesday to Sunday, 10am to 6pm
• Bus: 718

Symbols of secrecy and silence

A series of highly significant azulejos panels decorates the walls of *Madre de Deus* (Mother of God) church. This eastern part of Lisbon, of Braço de Prata or Lunar, was mainly inhabited by religious women and even some who had attained spiritual realisation, as was the case of some *beguines* of this very church, which made this a school of the hermetic tradition.

At the entrance, one of the doors bears the inscription RER, acronym of the Latin *Regina Eleonor Refacit* (Founded by Queen Leonor). Alchemically, RER also signifies the philosopher's vase where chemical transformations and sublimations of natural elements are carried out. It takes on the meaning of *Regeneratio*, as in the pious life of the martyr Santa Auta, represented with her chest pierced by an arrow, and whose remains have rested in this convent in a mother-of-pearl coffin since 2 September 1517.

The azulejo panels inside the church illustrate aspects of the religious life, not of the Franciscans, as might be expected in this Franciscan church, but of the Fathers of the Desert, like Saint Anthony the Hermit. Indeed, these hermits held the secrets of spiritual realisation, which required them to be silent, as is depicted on the portrait of a monk who clearly holds his index finger to his mouth (the panel at the back to the left of the altar).

Another large azulejo square shows the life of study, worship and work of the Fathers of the Desert, an allusion to the *lege, ora et labora* of the philosophers who practiced mystical alchemy, the strictly interior form (transformation of the lunar spirit into a solar spirit).

The path of spiritual realisation is represented by a long, wide alley lined with trees along which two figures, the master and the disciple, walk. Another panel depicts a cedar of Lebanon, the sacred tree representing the Tree of Life at the centre of the garden of Paradise (where a kneeling monk at prayer is surrounded by animals), here guarded by a crocodile, a symbol of the perfect disciple, incarnated by Saint Anthony, and the pope kneeling or in a position of submission at his feet, in the same way in which Peter bowed before John.

CHURCH OF SÃO FÉLIX DE CHELAS

Largo de Chelas, Marvila
• Visit by appointment. Contact the army archives on 218391600
• Bus: 104

> *The place where Ulysses came looking for Achilles?*

Still largely unknown (visits by appointment only), the church and convent of São Félix de Chelas have a rich and fabulous history that goes back to the time of the Greek hero Ulysses and his travelling companion, Achilles, and extends through the Visigoth period. It held so many objects to be admired or talked about that it became known as the "temple of marvels" and inspired the name *Maravilha* (Marvel), and also *Marvila*, which became the name of the neighbourhood. In an ambiance of miraculous legends, visitors can admire the relics of the church's 26 patron saints which in 1604 were placed in sculptures commissioned by Dona Luisa de Noronha, the convent's benefactor. They are exhibited on the altars of the church apse. There are also vestiges from the Roman occupation to be discovered, such as the famous *Sarcophagus of the Writers*, so-called because of the four muses (Thalia, Melpomene, Polyhymnia and Clio) who accompany the writer on the frieze. The Christian origin of the convent dates back to at least AD 665, when Recceswinth led the Visigoth monarchy. He supposedly received the relics of Saint Felix (tortured to death in Gerona in AD 30) by a boat that crossed the estuary that then covered the Chelas valley. In the 9th century, Afonso III of León took Lisbon from the Moors and gave the convent the relics of the martyrs Saint Adrian and his wife, Saint Natalia, that came from Galicia. In 1147, Dom Afonso Henriques rebuilt the edifice, had it consecrated again, and gave it to the Order of the Knights Templar, who became the beneficiaries of the entire Chelas valley and the eastern side of the city. In 1290, this religious building already belonged to the Order of Saint Augustine, which, up until 1219, maintained two reclusive communities here, one for men and one for women; only the female community survived. From 1757, archbishop Dom Miguel de Castro had the relics placed in chests donated by Dona Isabel Scota to the *Nascimento* (Birth) chapel, and placed below the entrance where mothers passed through with their sick babies to invoke the protection of the martyr saints, before then going to wash them in the water of a well located on the estuary's former quay. This former convent still has its Manueline gate, the atrium's polychrome azulejo panels, the cloister's fountain and benches with sloping backs, blue-and-white azulejo planters, and staircases covered in azulejos.

A temple of the vestal virgins dedicated to Thetis, queen of the Nereids (sea nymphs) or Tágides (Tagus nymphs), apparently stood at this same spot in the 7th century BC. According to legend, Ulysses came looking for Achilles who had taken refuge here, living dressed as a woman and probably participating in a sort of matriarchal initiation. *Achelas* and *Chelas* (which was also spelled *Celhas* during the reign of Dom João I) are supposedly derivatives of the name Achilles.

ALPHABETICAL INDEX

ALPHABETICAL INDEX

FIFTH EMPIRE

INDEX THEMATIC

HERMETISM

UNDERGROUND LISBON

SEBASTIANISM

SYMBOLS

KNIGHTS TEMPLAR

TRADITIONS

NOTES

NOTES

NOTES

Photography Credits

All photos were taken by **Paulo Andrade** with the exception of:

Rupert Eden: São Gens' chair, Symbols of the statue of King D. José I, Palace of Manteigueiro, Saint Catherine Church, the lizard of Penha de França, hermetic azulejos of Madre de Deus, the Dolls' hospital, the panels of the Restoration, the cistern of Saint Miguel de Alfama

Acknowledgements: Biblioteca Nacional de Lisboa, Dr.a Eneida Voss, Palácio Foz, Dr.a Sofia Carvalho, Associação Amigos dos Castelos, Dr. João Aníbal Henriques, Empresa Turística Tow, Patriarcado de Lisboa, Ministério do Exército, Câmara Municipal de Lisboa, Torre do Tombo, Museu Nacional de Arte Antiga, Museu Nacional de Arqueologia, Dr. Paulo Pereira (author of "Lugares Mágicos de Portugal", former president of IPPAR), Dr. Manuel J. Gandra (mythic history of Portugal), Professor Josué Pinharanda Gomes (pioneer of Portuguese philosophy), Museu da Cidade, Museu da Água, Comunidade Teúrgica Portuguesa, Dr. Juan Garcia Atienza (mythic history of Spain), Museu Maçónico Português, Geoffroy Moreno.

Maps: **Franz Huber**
Layout Design: **Roland Deloi**
Layout: **Stéphanie Benoit**
English Translation: **Kimberly Bess**
English Editing: **Caroline Lawrence**

© JONGLEZ 2010
Registration of copyright: June 2010 – Edition: 01
ISBN: 978-2-9158-0768-4
Printed in France by Mame - 37000 Tours